THE ESSENTIAL ROTHBARD

THE ESSENTIAL ROTHBARD

DAVID GORDON

Ludwig
von Mises
Institute
AUBURN, ALABAMA

ISBN: 10 digit: 1-933550-10-4
ISBN: 13 digit: 978-1-933550-10-7

CONTENTS

INTRODUCTION

Murray N. Rothbard, a scholar of extraordinary range, made major contributions to economics, history, political philosophy, and legal theory. He developed and extended the Austrian economics of Ludwig von Mises, in whose seminar he was a main participant for many years. He established himself as the principal Austrian theorist in the latter half of the twentieth century and applied Austrian analysis to topics such as the Great Depression of 1929 and the history of American banking.

A person examining the books and articles of Murray Rothbard without prior acquaintance with their author could not help wondering whether five or six prolific scholars shared the name "Murray Rothbard." Surely one man could not alone be the author of books in so many different academic fields, as well as hundreds of articles on contemporary politics. Anyone who had met Murray Rothbard, however, would experience no such bafflement at the scope of his immense intellectual productivity. His amazing mental quickness and energy made what would be a puzzle in almost anyone else a matter of course for him.

Rothbard was no ivory-tower scholar, interested only in academic controversies. Quite the contrary, he combined Austrian economics with a fervent commitment to individual liberty. He developed a unique synthesis that combined themes from nineteenth-century American individualists such as Lysander Spooner and Benjamin Tucker with Austrian economics. A new political philosophy was the result, and Rothbard devoted his remarkable intellectual energy, over a period of some 45 years, to developing and promoting his style of libertarianism. In doing so, he became a major American public intellectual.

I shall endeavor in what follows to provide a guide to the main lines of Rothbard's thought, through an account of his major books and a number of his articles.

THE EARLY YEARS—
BECOMING A LIBERTARIAN

Murray Rothbard was born March 2, 1926, the son of David and Rae Rothbard. He was a brilliant student even as a young child; and his academic record at Columbia University, where he majored in mathematics and economics, was stellar.

At Columbia, the philosopher Ernest Nagel impressed Rothbard a great deal. Nagel was always ready to engage students in discussion: Rothbard said that he always appeared eager to learn whether a student could contribute to a problem that was puzzling him. Nagel stressed careful analysis of arguments; and in a class that Rothbard attended on the philosophy of the social sciences, Nagel criticized the institutionalist school for its opposition to economic theory. Nagel maintained that economists should not confine themselves to amassing data. A good theory explains the facts: it does not just reproduce them.

If so, the main objection of the institutionalists to economic laws failed. They claimed that theoretical statements were inevitably only approximately true, since they can never reproduce with full accuracy the details of the real world.

> Institutionalists conceive of economic theory as only relative to *particular historical situations*; therefore universal economic theoretical laws are illegitimate. According to the institutionalists, each theorist discourses on the most pressing problems of his day. . . . So they conclude that economic theorists are selective. But any scientific inquiry is selective![1]

---

[1]Lecture notes from Ernest Nagel's class, taken by Rothbard in the summer of 1948; Rothbard Papers. The Murray N. Rothbard Papers are held at the Ludwig von Mises Institute in Auburn, Alabama, and include Rothbard's letters, correspondence (1940–1995), memos and unpublished essays (1945–1994), and drafts of published works, as well as Old Right and libertarian movement papers.

Nagel admitted the premise but denied the conclusion. An explanation does not aim to reproduce the world, just to account for it. If the economist says, e.g., that under certain conditions, if the price of a good falls, the quantity demanded will increase, his explanation cannot be faulted for failure to list every detail about each particular market.

> A theory must: (1) *explain*, (2) *afford means for prediction*. . . . To criticize a theory (as do the institutionalists) on the ground that the fundamental assumptions are not supported by statistical evidence is very weak—it takes centuries to accumulate evidence.[2]

Rothbard absorbed Nagel's point about explanation and never deviated from it; but he soon came to reject Nagel's views on prediction.

In accepting theory, he differed with the teaching of most of the faculty of the Columbia economics department. Many of the most important professors accepted the institutionalist creed. Heavily influenced by Wesley Clair Mitchell, the key figure in the National Bureau of Economic Research, Arthur Burns and John Maurice Clark looked at economic theory skeptically.[3] Burns was himself an excellent theorist, but his skills were mainly directed to the criticism of the work of others.[4] Burns had known Rothbard since he was a child, and David Rothbard asked Burns to "look out" for his

---

[2]Notes from Nagel lectures; Rothbard Papers.

[3]Nagel criticized Mitchell in his lectures; Rothbard Papers.

[4]In *Man, Economy, and State*, Rothbard credits Burns for an important criticism of the theory of monopolistic competition, presented in his classroom lectures. In 2004, as Rothbard had originally intended, *Man, Economy, and State* was published together with *Power and Market*. All quotations and page references here are from this edition, *Man, Economy, and State with Power and Market*, Scholar's Edition (1962; Auburn, Ala.: Ludwig von Mises Institute, 2004), p. 732.

son. No close academic relationship ever developed between the two during Rothbard's stay at Columbia, however.

Fortunately, one of his teachers, George Stigler, was not averse to theory; and in his lectures Rothbard encountered arguments critical of price and rent control that much impressed him. Stigler, together with Milton Friedman, had written a pamphlet critical of price control, published by the Foundation for Economic Education.[5] Rothbard wrote to this group and soon visited their headquarters. Here he met FEE's founder, Leonard Read, as well as F.A. ("Baldy") Harper, an economist and social philosopher who not only supported the free market, but also doubted the need for a government at all. Even more significantly, he met Ludwig von Mises. Mises's rigorous defense of free market economics had a profound effect on Rothbard's thinking; and when Mises's masterwork, *Human Action*,[6] appeared in 1949, he devoured the book. He joined Mises's seminar at New York University, becoming one of its main participants. For the seminar, he wrote a number of papers that he later in part incorporated into his published work: these included a report on the neo-Kantian economist Harro Bernardelli's criticism of utility theory and an analysis of the quantity theory of money.

Meanwhile, Rothbard had graduated from Columbia—he was elected a member of Phi Beta Kappa—with a major in economics and mathematics and had begun graduate work in economics.[7]

---

[5]George Stigler and Milton Friedman, *Roofs or Ceilings?: The Current Housing Problem* (Irvington-on-Hudson, N.Y.: Foundation for Economic Education, 1946).

[6]Ludwig von Mises, *Human Action: A Treatise on Economics*, Scholar's Edition (1949; Auburn, Ala.: Ludwig von Mises Institute, 1998).

[7]Critics of Austrian economics who allege that the school's reluctance to use mathematics stems from the inability of Austrians to cope with the subject should note that Rothbard was an excellent mathematician. He especially liked set theory.

In graduate school, Rothbard's mentor was the eminent economic historian Joseph Dorfman, the author of the multivolume *The Economic Mind in American Civilization*,[8] a work of vast erudition. Rothbard said of him:

> Prof. Dorfman is absolutely without peer as a pure scholar in the history of American economic thought and opinion. He makes most historians seem like journalists. . . . Dorfman was the first one to annihilate Arthur Schlesinger, Jr.'s *Age of Jackson*. Schlesinger had presented Jackson as a proto-FDR, leading the forces of the masses against monopoly capitalism; actually, Dorfman showed that the Jacksonians were libertarian types: favoring free trade, *laissez-faire*, states' rights, and hard money, and were pro-commerce.[9]

Rothbard shared Dorfman's passion for historical learning, and his Ph.D. thesis on *The Panic of 1819*[10] remains to this day a standard work. Rothbard received his doctorate in 1956; he could not finish earlier owing to disagreements between Dorfman and Burns about how the thesis should proceed.

As he deepened his understanding of *laissez-faire* economics, he confronted a dilemma. If sound arguments showed that the market could supply goods and services better than the State could, why should one make an exception for defense and justice? Why here do we face a unique situation in which provision by a coercive monopoly outperforms the market? The arguments for market provision of goods and services applied across the board. If so, should not even protection and defense be offered on the market rather than supplied by a coercive monopoly? Rothbard realized that he would either have to reject *laissez-faire* or embrace individualist anarchism. The decision, arrived at in the winter of 1949,

---

[8]Joseph Dorfman, *The Economic Mind in American Civilization*, 5 vols. (New York: Viking Press, 1946).

[9]Letter to Ivan Bierly, November 14, 1959; Rothbard Papers.

[10]*The Panic of 1819* (New York: Columbia University Press, 1962).

was not difficult. Once the issue was raised, Rothbard realized that, however surprising it might seem, the free market need not be abandoned even here.

In arriving at his iconoclastic response, Rothbard was much influenced by several nineteenth-century individualist anarchists. He called Lysander Spooner's *No Treason*[11] "the greatest case for anarchist political philosophy ever written," listing it under "Books That Formed Me."[12] He termed Benjamin Tucker a "brilliant political philosopher" despite his "abysmal ignorance of economics."[13] The detailed attempt by the Belgian economist Gustave de Molinari to spell out how a system of private protection would work impressed him:

> In short, he reasoned: [if] free competition [can] supply consumers with the most efficient service, and monopoly was always bad in all other goods and services, why should this not apply to the service of defense. He maintained that single entrepreneurs would be able to supply protection in the rural districts, while large insurance type companies could supply the urban consumers.[14]

[11]Lysander Spooner, *No Treason* (Larkspur, Colo.: Pine Tree Press, 1965).

[12]Memo to Tom Fleming, January 24, 1994; Rothbard Papers.

[13]Unpublished essay, "A Reply by Benjamin Tucker II," undated, c. 1954; Rothbard Papers.

[14]"On Gustave de Molinari," unpublished, no date; Rothbard Papers.

MAN, ECONOMY, AND STATE: ROTHBARD'S TREATISE ON ECONOMIC THEORY

R othbard soon attracted the attention of the William Volker Fund, at that time the leading group that gave financial aid to classical-liberal scholars. It commissioned Rothbard to write a textbook, suitable for college students, which would explain *Human Action* in simple language. He wrote a sample chapter on money and credit that won Mises's approval. As Rothbard's work proceeded, the project turned into something much larger. The result, the two-volume *Man, Economy, and State*, was a major treatise, published in 1962, and, one of the most important twentieth-century contributions to Austrian economics.

Mises recognized the book's importance. Reviewing it in *The New Individualist Review*, Mises called it "an epochal contribution to the general science of human action, praxeology, and its practically most important and up-to-now best elaborated part, economics."[15] Mises, as any student of his work knows, was a formidable critic; for him to say this about a book is genuinely remarkable.

Rothbard was entirely in accord with Mises's endeavor to deduce the whole of economics from the axiom of action, combined with a few subsidiary postulates. In much more detail than Mises had done, he carried out the deduction; and in the process, he contributed major theoretical innovations to praxeology.

His view of praxeology differed in a subtle but substantial way from that of Mises. Rothbard thought that we directly grasp necessities in the empirical world. Not only do we see that human beings act: we at the same time understand that this is a necessary

---

[15]Ludwig von Mises, *The New Individualist Review* (Autumn, 1962): 41.

feature of human nature. This is an Aristotelian and Scholastic view, in contrast with Mises's Kantian position; when stating that "all human beings *act* by virtue of their existence and their nature as human beings", Rothbard cites in support Book I of Aristotle's *Nicomachean Ethics*.[16] Mises contended that human beings have to think according to certain categories. If so, we can know certain propositions, like the action axiom, to be true *a priori*; we know these propositions in the sense that we cannot think in a way that contradicts them. This allows a gap between the world as it appears to us and the world as it is in itself. No such gap exists in Rothbard's view.

He rejected the standard neoclassical use of mathematical proof in economics, a point that was not lost on Mises, who commented:

> In a few brilliant lines, he [Rothbard] demolishes the main device of mathematical economists, viz., the fallacious idea of substituting the concepts of mutual determination and equilibrium for the allegedly outdated concept of cause and effect.[17]

The work was remarkable for its rigor and creativity. One of the most important of the book's innovations involved a famous argument of Mises. Rothbard maintained that Mises's socialist calculation argument was not, in essence, an argument about socialism at all. Rather, the fundamental point of the argument was that in the absence of the market, economic calculation could not take place. Thus, a single firm, even if privately owned, that controlled an entire economy would likewise be unable to calculate:

> Our analysis serves to expand the famous discussion of the possibility of economic calculation under socialism, launched by Professor Ludwig von Mises over 40 years ago. Mises, who has had the last as well as the first word in the debate,

---

[16]*Man, Economy, and State with Power and Market*, p. 2.

[17]Mises, *New Individualist Review*, p. 40.

has demonstrated irrefutably that a socialist economic system cannot calculate, since it lacks a market, and hence lacks prices for producers' and especially for capital goods. Now we see that, paradoxically, the reason why a socialist economy cannot calculate is *not* specifically because it is socialist! Socialism is that system in which the state forcibly seizes control of all the means of production in the economy. The reason for the impossibility of calculation under socialism is that *one agent* owns or directs the use of all the resources in the economy. It should be clear that it does not make any difference whether that one agent is the State or one private individual or private cartel. Whichever occurs, there is no possibility of calculation anywhere in the production structure, since production processes would be only internal and without markets. There could be no calculation, and therefore complete economic irrationality and chaos would prevail, whether the single owner is the State or private persons.[18]

Rothbard here brilliantly combined Mises's argument with a central contention of Ronald Coase's "The Nature of the Firm."[19] Coase considered individual firms, faced with the decision whether to extend production internally or buy products on the market. He said that in "a competitive system there is an 'optimum' amount of planning."[20] Rothbard saw that Mises and Coase were making a similar point. As Rothbard notes,

> *For every capital good, there must be a definite market in which firms buy and sell that good.* It is obvious that this economic law *sets a definite maximum to the relative size of any particular firm on the free market.* . . . Because of this law, there can never be One Big Cartel over the whole economy or mergers until One Big Firm owns all the productive assets in the economy.[21]

---

[18]*Man, Economy, and State with Power and Market*, pp. 614–15.

[19]Ronald Coase, "The Nature of the Firm," *Economica* n.s. 386 (1937).

[20]Quoted in *Man, Economy, and State with Power and Market*, p. 613.

[21]Ibid., p. 613; emphasis in the original.

No tendency toward monopoly existed on the free market. Here Rothbard followed Mises and other free market economists; but he went beyond them. In another innovation, he claimed that the entire concept of monopoly price did not apply to the free market. No means exists to distinguish a so-called monopoly price, charged by a single firm in an industry, from a competitive price.

> [T]here has been a great deficiency in the economic literature on this whole issue: a failure to realize *the illusion in the entire concept of monopoly price . . . that there is assumed to be* a "competitive price," to which a higher "monopoly price"—an outcome of restrictive action—is contrasted. Yet, if we analyze the matter closely, it becomes evident that . . . there is no way of distinguishing, even conceptually, any given price as a "monopoly price." The alleged "competitive price" can be identified neither by the producer himself nor by the disinterested observer.[22]

Rothbard's argument for this radical conclusion was straightforward:

> Neither does the elasticity of the demand curve establish any criterion. Even if all the difficulties of discovering and identifying the demand curve were waived . . . we have seen that the price, if accurately estimated, will always be set by the sellers so that the *range above the market price will be elastic.* How is anyone, including the producer himself, to know whether or not this market price is competitive or monopoly?[23]

He shows no mercy to the monopolistic competition theories of Joan Robinson and Edward Chamberlin:

> The monopolistic-competition theorist contrasts this ideal firm [i.e., one without influence on price] with those firms that have some influence on the determination of price and are therefore in some degree "monopolistic." Yet it is obvious

---

[22]Ibid., pp. 687–88; emphasis in the original.

[23]Ibid., p. 689; emphasis in the original.

that the demand curve to a firm *cannot* be perfectly elastic throughout.[24]

Capital theory is central to Austrian economics, and Rothbard attaches especial importance to his unification of Frank Fetter's "brilliant and neglected theory of rent"[25] with the pure time preference theory of interest and the Austrian theory of the structure of production. It is hardly surprising that he was keen to show the advantages of the Austrian view against competing doctrines, and he gives a penetrating criticism of the main alternative position. According to Frank Knight, capital is a perpetual fund; this contrasts with the Austrian view, pioneered by Eugen von Böhm-Bawerk, that stresses the stages of production over time. Rothbard assails this theory in the form given to it by one of Knight's disciples, Earl Rolph.

> Let Rolph picture a production system, atomized or integrated as the case may be, with no one making the advances of present goods (money capital) that he denies exist. And as the laborers and landowners work on the intermediate products for years without pay, until the finished product is ready for the consumer, let Rolph exhort them not to worry, since they have been implicitly paid simultaneously as they worked. For this is the logical implication of the Knight-Rolph position.[26]

Rothbard offers a fundamental and far reaching criticism of Keynesian economics. He begins his assault on Keynes by pointing out that at the basis of the entire Keynesian system is a false assumption. Keynes maintained that total spending could fall short of what is needed to maintain full employment. But how can this be? If workers are unemployed, will they not bid down wages? How then can there be continued unemployment on the free market?

---

[24]Ibid., p. 721; emphasis in the original.

[25]Ibid., p. xcv.

[26]Ibid., p. 507.

Keynes assumed that wages could not fall. "The Keynesian 'underemployment equilibrium' occurs only *if money wage rates are rigid downward*, i.e., if the supply curve of labor below 'full employment' is infinitely elastic."[27]

By an increase in government spending, while money wages remain constant, real wages drop. Keynes's much vaunted innovation consists of an elaborate attempt to trick workers. They look only to their money wages; somehow, they will fail to notice that they face a wage cut.

Rothbard finds the Keynesian prescription totally inadequate:

> Unions, however, have learned about purchasing-power problems and the distinction between money and real rates; indeed, it hardly requires much reasoning ability to grasp this distinction. Ironically, Keynes' advocacy of inflation based on the "money illusion" rested on the historical experience . . . that, during an inflation, selling prices rise faster than wage rates. Yet an economy in which unions impose minimum wage rates is precisely an economy in which unions will be alive to any losses in their real, as well as their money, wages.[28]

To end unemployment, then, wages must fall. But the Keynesians are not yet defeated: they "fall back on one last string in their bow."[29] They argue that even if wages do fall, unemployment can persist. The speculative demand to hold cash will block investment: businessmen, anticipating a drop in prices, will hoard their money.

Rothbard's analysis of this idea is one of his foremost innovations. In his criticism, he anticipated the work on rational expectations for which Robert Lucas later won the Nobel Prize.[30]

---

[27]Ibid., p. 780.

[28]Ibid., p. 784.

[29]Ibid., p. 785.

[30]I am grateful to Professor Bryan Caplan for calling this to my attention.

Rothbard maintains that Keynes wrongly thinks that the speculative demand to hold money determines the rate of interest. Instead, the demand to hold money is a speculative response:

> One grave and fundamental Keynesian error is to persist in regarding the interest rate as a contract rate on loans, instead of the price spreads between stages of production. The former, as we have seen, is only the reflection of the latter. A strong expectation of a rapid rise in interest rate means a strong expectation of an increase in the price spreads, or rate of net return. A fall in prices means that entrepreneurs expect that factor prices will fall *further* in the near future than their selling prices . . . all we are confronted with is a situation in which entrepreneurs, expecting that factor prices will soon fall, cease investing and wait for this happy event so that their return will be greater. This is *not* "liquidity preference," but *speculation on price changes*.[31]

At this point, Rothbard advances the crucial point that anticipates Lucas. He argues that such speculation is not a source of instability. To the contrary, the "expectation of falling factor prices speeds up the movement toward equilibrium and hence toward the pure interest relation as determined by time preference."[32]

But what if the demand to hold money increases to an unlimited extent? What if entrepreneurs do not invest at all? Rothbard again counters with a "rational expectations" point:

> The Keynesian worry is that people will hoard instead of buying bonds for fear of a fall on the price of securities . . . this would mean . . . not investing because of expectation of imminent increases in the natural interest rate. Rather than act as a blockade, however, this expectation *speeds* the ensuing adjustment. Furthermore, the demand for money could not be infinite since people must always continue consuming, whatever their expectations.[33]

---

[31]*Man, Economy, and State with Power and Market*, pp. 789–90; emphasis in the original.

[32]Ibid., p. 790.

[33]Ibid., p. 791.

In sum, the Keynesian view of liquidity preference is fundamentally inadequate:

> Keynesians, however, attribute liquidity preference, not to *general* uncertainty, but to the specific uncertainty of future bond prices. Surely this is a highly superficial and limiting view.[34]

Rothbard's point about the role of expectations in speeding adjustment of the interest rate applies more widely than to the Keynesian problem of hoarding. The effect is present for all anticipated price changes. He writes:

> [T]he natural interest rate on the market has contained a *purchasing-power component*, which corrects for real rates, positively in money terms during a general expansion, and negatively during a general contraction. The loan rate will be simply a reflection of what has been happening in the natural rate. So far, the discussion is similar to [Irving] Fisher's, except that these are the results of *actual*, not anticipated changes. . . . We have seen that rather than take a monetary loss . . . entrepreneurs will hold back their purchases of factors until factor prices fall immediately to their future low level. But this process of anticipatory price movement does not occur only in the extreme case of a prospective "negative" return. *It happens whenever a price change is anticipated.* . . . If all changes were anticipated by everyone, there would be no room for a purchasing-power component [of the rate of interest] to develop.[35]

---

[34]Ibid.; emphasis in the original.

[35]Ibid., p. 796.

POWER AND MARKET:
THE FINAL PART OF ROTHBARD'S TREATISE

As Rothbard originally planned *Man, Economy, and State*, it was to include a final part that presented a comprehensive classification and analysis of types of government intervention. Unfortunately, this part of the book appeared in the original edition only in a severely truncated form. Its full publication came only in 1970, under the title *Power and Market*.[36] The complete version of *Man, Economy, and State with Power and Market*, as Rothbard originally intended it to appear, was finally published in 2004.

In *Power and Market*, he divides intervention into two types: triangular, in which "the invader compels a pair of people to make an exchange or prohibits them from doing so,"[37] and binary, which is a coerced exchange between the invader and his victim (taxation is the principal example of this). With great care, he elaborates a detailed classification of the possible sorts of intervention that fall under each heading, in every case showing the deleterious effects of such interference.

As one illustration of Rothbard in action, consider the following:

> All government expenditure for resources is a form of *consumption* expenditure, in the sense that the money is spent on various items because the government officials so decree. . . . It is true that the officials do not consume the product directly, *but their wish* has altered the production pattern to make these goods, and therefore they may be called "consumers" . . . all talk of government "investment" is fallacious.[38]

---

[36]*Power and Market: Government and the Economy* (Kansas City: Sheed Andrews and McMeel, 1970).

[37]*Man, Economy, and State with Power and Market*, p. 1075.

[38]Ibid., p. 1153.

A simple, even self-evident point, once Rothbard has called it to our attention, but it was hardly very obvious to previous writers.

Power and Market does not contain Rothbard's ethical system; it is a work of praxeology and is thus value free. Nevertheless, Rothbard maintains that the praxeologist can arrive at conclusions highly relevant to ethics. If a proposed ethical ideal cannot be realized, it must rationally be rejected. To accept this requires no adherence to a particular ethical view: it is a requirement of reason.

> If an ethical goal can be shown to be self-contradictory and *conceptually impossible* of fulfillment, then the goal is clearly an absurd one and should be abandoned by all . . . *it is equally absurd to take measures to approach that ideal* . . . this is a praxeological truth derived from the law that a means can obtain its value only by being imputed from the end.[39]

One such impossible goal is equality of income.

> Income can *never* be equal. Income must be considered, of course, in real and not in money terms; otherwise there would be no true equality. . . . Since every individual is necessarily situated in a different space, every individual's real income must differ from good to good and from person to person. There is no way to combine goods of different types, to measure some income "level," so it is meaningless to try to arrive at some sort of "equal" level.[40]

Equality of opportunity fares no better.

> Yet this, too, is as meaningless as the former concept. How can the New Yorker's opportunity and the Indian's opportunity to sail around Manhattan, or to swim the Ganges, be "equalized"? Man's inevitable diversity of location effectively eliminates any possibility of equalizing "opportunity."[41]

---

[39]Ibid., pp. 1297–98.
[40]Ibid., p. 1310.
[41]Ibid.

The book also subjected to withering criticism the standard canons of justice in taxation. Rothbard's line of attack differed from that of most of free market economists, who emphasized the evils of progressive taxation. Rothbard had no love for the progressive principle, but he found some of the arguments against it to be flawed:

> The . . . objection is a political-ethical one—that "the poor rob the rich." The implication is that the poor man who pays 1 percent of his income is "robbing" the rich man who pays 80 percent. Without judging the merits or demerits of robbery, we may say that this is invalid. *Both* citizens are being robbed—by the State. . . . It may be objected that the poor receive a net subsidy out of the tax proceeds . . . [but] [t]he fact of progressive taxation does not *itself* imply that "the poor" en masse will be subsidized.[42]

To Rothbard, the level of taxation is the key issue: "Actually, the *level* of taxation is far more important than its progressiveness in determining the distance a society has traveled from the free market."[43] A rich person required to pay a steeply progressive tax would be better off than under a proportional system with higher rates.

A brief but brilliant passage refuted in advance the antimarket arguments based on "luck" that were to prove so influential in the later work of John Rawls and his many successors.

> [T]here is no justification for saying that the rich are luckier than the poor. It might very well be that many or most of the rich have been *unlucky* and are getting less than their true DMVP [discounted marginal value product], while most of the poor have been *lucky* and are getting more. No one can say what the distribution of luck is; hence, there is no justification here for a "redistribution" policy.[44]

---

[42]Ibid., pp. 1193–94.

[43]Ibid., p. 1194.

[44]Ibid., p. 1333. The philosopher Susan Hurley later developed the same point in her *Justice, Luck, and Knowledge* (Cambridge, Mass.:

Rothbard's point does not depend on accepting his view that people deserve to get the value of what they produce. Rather, the issue is that one must first specify a principle of distribution before one can tell whether someone is "lucky."

Advocates of the free market contend that the private charity would suffice for the poor and disabled, but they must here respond to an objection. Is not charity degrading? Rothbard's reply remains within the confines of praxeology, since it involves no appeal to ethical judgments. He notes that someone who raises this objection cannot consistently support government aid.

> Statists . . . often argue that charity is demeaning and degrading to the recipient, and that he should therefore be taught that the money is rightly his, to be given to him by the government as his due. But this oft-felt degradation stems, as Isabel Paterson pointed out, from the fact that the recipient of charity is not self-supporting on the market. . . . However, granting him the moral and legal right to mulct his fellows *increases* his moral degradation instead of ending it, for the beneficiary is now further removed from the production line than ever. . . . [W]e simply say that anyone who considers private charity degrading must logically conclude that State charity is far more so.[45]

Harvard University Press, 2003). See my review in *The Mises Review* 9, no. 2 (Summer, 2003).

[45]Ibid., pp. 1320–21.

MORE ADVANCES IN ECONOMIC THEORY:
THE LOGIC OF ACTION

Rothbard's masterly work, *Man, Economy, and State*, was far from exhausting his contributions to economic theory. Rothbard's main papers in this area are available in the posthumously published two-volume collection *The Logic of Action*.[46]

A constant theme echoes again and again throughout Rothbard's papers. He found it essential to separate the distinctive Austrian approach to economics from competing views, not least from movements within Austrian economics that he believed were misguided. One motive for this essential work of clarification is that economics is a strict science; as such, it must be purged of all that does not properly belong to it. In particular, ethical judgments do not form part of economic analysis: "[E]ven the tritest bits of ethical judgments in economics are completely illegitimate."[47] Rothbard held this view not because he thought ethics a matter of arbitrary whim. Quite the contrary, in "Praxeology: the Methodology of Austrian Economics" (1976),[48] he calls himself an Aristotelian Neo-Thomist, and this school ardently champions natural law. But whatever the scientific status of ethics, economics is an independent discipline.

And the issue is more than one of conceptual economy and elegance. Though ethics need not be capricious, many economists do

---

[46]*The Logic of Action I: Method, Money, and the Austrian School* (Cheltenham, U.K.: Edward Elgar, 1997). *The Logic of Action II: Applications and Criticism from the Austrian School* (Cheltenham, U.K.: Edward Elgar, 1997. The two volumes are included in Edward Elgar's series Economists of the Twentieth Century. A new and expanded edition will be published by the Ludwig von Mises Institute in 2007.

[47]*Logic of Action I*, p. 22.

[48]Ibid., pp. 58–99.

in fact lack any rational basis for their ethical views. By importing their unsupported preferences into their work, they throw science overboard. "[I]t is the responsibility of any scientist, indeed any intellectual, to refrain from any value judgment whatever *unless* he can support it on the basis of a coherent and defensible ethical system."[49]

This statement itself expresses a value judgment; but since the statement can be coherently supported, Rothbard has not contradicted himself by asserting it.

But how can the offending economists commit so gross a fallacy? Are they not aware that the ethical premises they use throw into question the standing of their work as scientific? Rothbard offers an answer in "Toward a Reconstruction of Utility and Welfare Economics" (1956),[50] one of his most brilliant essays. Conventional welfare economists reasoned in this way: Ethical judgments are, admittedly, arbitrary. But surely there exist noncontroversial judgments—truisms that everyone will accept. In particular, if a policy maximizes welfare, ought it not to be adopted?

But, as mainstream economists recognized, no solution lay here in sight. Comparisons of utility among different persons, it was almost universally agreed, could not be made; how then could one determine whether a proposed measure did advance welfare better than any available alternative? And was the goal of maximum welfare genuinely uncontroversial? Nearly every policy will make some better off, while harming others. Even if welfare could be measured, on what scientific basis can one say that the losers should give way to the winners?

Ever resourceful, the so-called new welfare economists thought they had discovered a solution. Suppose a policy makes at least one person better off, while worsening no one. Could one not then endorse this policy without making any controversial value judgments? A rule that no one can rationally controvert, the Pareto criterion, offers a foothold for a scientific welfare economics.

---

[49]Ibid., p. 82.
[50]Ibid., pp. 211–54.

But the conclusions of the new welfare economics, in line with the dominant interventionism of twentieth-century social science, brought little comfort to supporters of the free market. Market imperfections, stemming from positive and negative externalities, required the state constantly to intervene.

Rothbard will have none of this. In a veritable *tour de force*, he argues that the assumptions of welfare economics, if correctly interpreted, lend support to the free market. An economist, acting in his purely scientific capacity, can take account only of consumer preferences demonstrated in action. And if he abides by this restriction, he will of necessity condemn every governmental interference with voluntary trade.

As the same essay illustrates, Rothbard took nothing for granted in ethics. Much of conventional welfare economics depends on the detection of positive externalities. Rothbard, with his characteristic jump to the essence, inquires, why are positive externalities a social problem?

> A and B decide to pay for the building of a dam for their use; C benefits though he did not pay. . . . This is the problem of the Free Rider. Yet it is difficult to understand what the hullabaloo is all about. Am I to be specially taxed because I enjoy the sight of my neighbor's garden without paying for it? A's and B's purchase of a good reveals that *they* are willing to pay for it; if it indirectly benefits C as well, no one is the loser.[51]

In "The Fallacy of the Public Sector" (1961),[52] he exposes the central mistake in the external benefits argument in even more memorable fashion:

> A and B often benefit, it is held, if they can force C into doing something. . . . [S]uffice it to say here that any argument proclaiming the right and goodness of, say, three neighbors, who yearn to form a string quartet, forcing a fourth neighbor at

---

[51]*Logic of Action I*, p. 251.
[52]*Logic of Action II*, pp. 171–79.

bayonet point to learn and play the viola, is hardly deserving
of sober comment.[53]

Let us pause to grasp the revolution involved in Rothbard's
query. Before him economists assumed without much thought that
beneficiaries of positive externalities ought to pay for them. Once
Rothbard had raised the question, one cannot help but wonder,
why should the conventional premise be assumed without argument? When Robert Nozick made a similar point in *Anarchy,
State, and Utopia*,[54] philosophers were quick to take notice. But
Rothbard was there long before.

Some might respond to Rothbard by arguing that it maximizes
efficiency for beneficiaries of positive externalities to pay for them.
Rothbard blocks this move with a challenge to the entire concept
of efficiency.

Everyone knows that the free market is the most efficient economic system; Milton Friedman and his many disciples build their
defense of the market largely on this consideration. One might
expect that Rothbard, second to none as a champion of the market,
would join in lauding its efficiency. Instead, he asks a fundamental
question: does the concept of efficiency mean anything?

> Let us take a given individual . . . in order for him to act effi-
> ciently, he would have to possess perfect knowledge of the
> future. . . . But since no one can ever have perfect knowledge
> of the future, no one's action can be called "efficient." . . . [I]f
> ends change in the course of an action, the concept of effi-
> ciency—which can be defined as the best combination of
> means in pursuit of given ends—again becomes meaning-
> less.[55]

---

[53]Ibid., p. 178.

[54]Robert Nozick, *Anarchy, State, and Utopia* (New York: Basic Books,
1974), pp. 93–94.

[55]*Logic of Action* I, pp. 266–67.

Murray Rothbard viewed the logical positivists with alarm; but as the example just given shows, he used with great skill a favorite tactic of theirs. He asks: what is the operational definition of a concept under discussion? If none can be provided, the concept—in this instance, efficiency—must be eliminated from science.[56]

Rothbard did not contend that he had offered a value-neutral defense of the market. Rather, he turned the weapons of the interventionists against themselves; in so doing, he showed how important it is to be on the alert for ethical judgments assumed without argument. But to say that ethics must be separated from economics of course leaves open a major issue: what is the correct method of economics?

Rothbard's answer was of course that economics proceeds from simple, common sense axioms, in particular the "axiom of action." His work in economic method won the praise of Friedrich Hayek, who remarked: "Professor Rothbard's writings are undoubtedly most helpful contributions to a great tradition."[57]

The deductive method of procedure, exemplified in Mises's praxeology, must battle two principal adversaries. The first of these rightly takes economics as a science, but has an overly constricted view of scientific method. To positivists, physics is the model science, and economics must ape that discipline's use of testable hypotheses. Rothbard, in his classic essay "The Mantle of Science" (1960), condemns this approach as a "profoundly unscientific attempt to transfer uncritically the methodology of the physical sciences to the study of human action."[58] By seeking to force economics into the Procrustean bed of physics, as conceived of by positivists, the proponents of scientism ignore free will.

---

[56]Another instance of the same technique may be found in the search for an operational definition of monopoly price in *Man, Economy, and State*. I suspect, but cannot prove, the influence of his teacher Ernest Nagel for this technique.

[57]F.A. Hayek, "Foreword" to Rothbard's, *Individualism and the Philosophy of the Social Sciences* (San Francisco: Cato Paper No. 4), p. x.

[58]*Logic of Action I*, p. 3.

However dangerous scientism may be, its blandishments are unlikely to attract those sympathetic to Austrian economics. Rothbard issues a call to arms against a more immediate threat in "The Present State of Austrian Economics" (1992).[59] As everyone knows, Austrian value theory is subjective: Austrians explain prices through individual preferences and reject the Marxist labor theory of value and other such accounts. But some professed Austrians have gone too far. To them, everything is subjective and economics as a science dissolves. Following Ludwig Lachmann, they stress the radical uncertainty of the future. Austrian economics, as Rothbard practices it, must not be equated with the endless repetition of the words "subjectivism" and "uncertainty."

As mentioned in the discussion of *Man, Economy, and State*, Rothbard made important contributions to the socialist calculation argument; and the collection adds several essential papers on the topic. In "The End of Socialism and the Calculation Debate Revisited" (1991), he notes, against Hayek and Kirzner, that "the central problem [of socialism] is not 'knowledge'."[60] No doubt, as Hayek emphasized, there is a knowledge problem under socialism; a centrally planning agency cannot amass the incredibly complex information required to run a modern economy. But, to reiterate, the key problem is not, how do you obtain knowledge? Rather, it is what do you do with the knowledge, once you have it? And here calculation, and with it the market, plays its indispensable role.

In "Lange, Mises, and Praxeology: The Retreat from Marxism" (1971),[61] Rothbard appends an amusing footnote to the calculation debate. The most famous socialist opponent of Mises and Hayek was the Polish economist Oskar Lange. Yet toward the end of his life, Lange, though unwavering in his commitment to socialism, wound up as a champion of praxeology. In an effort to separate his views from those of his great antagonist Mises, Lange endeavored

[59]Ibid., pp. 111–72.
[60]Ibid., p. 425.
[61]Ibid., pp. 384–96.

to combine praxeology with Marxism—surely an unstable compound.

The reader of "Applications and Criticism from the Austrian School," volume II of *The Logic of Action*, will carry away an overwhelming impression of the variety of topics in which Rothbard was interested; and only a few essays can be singled out here for mention. Just as in the first volume. Rothbard's insistence on conceptual clarity is everywhere to the fore.

In "The Fallacy of the Public Sector," he demolishes John Kenneth Galbraith's polemic against capitalism with a single question that strikes to the jugular. Galbraith endeavored to answer the standard argument that capitalism best serves the needs of consumers. No doubt, Galbraith conceded, a free market provides an abundance of goods—but is this not just the problem? These goods do not meet the genuine needs of consumers, but desires for them are whipped up artificially through advertising. Rothbard inquires, "*Is* everything above subsistence 'artificial'?"[62]

So much for Galbraith. In "The Myth of Tax 'Reform'" (1981),[63] Rothbard uses his analytical tools to lend clarity to an issue of dominant concern. The essential point about taxation, Rothbard again and again stresses, is that it is coercive: it is a compulsory exaction of resources from the productive sectors of the economy. Many economists view taxation as if it were a voluntary agreement for the provision of so-called "public goods." Reverting to a point made in his fundamental essay on welfare economics, Rothbard refuses to countenance in economic science alleged preferences not expressed on the free market. Genuinely voluntary action, not the counterfeit of "voluntary" taxation, can provide for defense and protection.

He extends his criticism of voluntary taxation to the most famous text of the influential Public Choice School, James

---

[62]*Logic of Action II*, p. 177.
[63]Ibid., pp. 109–20.

Buchanan and Gordon Tullock's *The Calculus of Consent*,[64] in "Buchanan and Tullock's *The Calculus of Consent*."[65] To support their odd notion that likens the state to a club, these authors appeal to unanimous action. If everyone agrees to be taxed, is not the enforcement of this agreement in accord with popular will? Rothbard unerringly locates the fallacy of this contention. Buchanan and Tullock in fact retreat from complete unanimity in their constitutional requirements, owing to transaction costs. If so, they cannot rightly appeal to that very unanimity in their attempt to turn coercion into freedom. Rothbard located this crucial fallacy in *The Calculus of Consent* before it was published, in comments on the manuscript.

He elaborated his objection in "Toward a Reconstruction of Utility and Welfare Economics." Buchanan's attempt

> to designate the State as a voluntary institution . . . is based on the curious dialectic that majority rule in a democracy is really unanimity because majorities can and do always shift! The resulting pulling and hauling of the political process, because obviously not irreversible, are therefore supposed to yield a social unanimity. The doctrine . . . must be set down as a lapse into a type of Hegelian mysticism.[66]

Rothbard's procedure is a simple one. He asks: what does the voluntary state amount to? And given Buchanan's characterization of it, Rothbard goes on to ask: is this what we ordinarily mean by "voluntary"? As it obviously is not, this conception of the voluntary state cannot stand.

Ever alert for semantic evasion, Rothbard maintained that it is inaccurate to refer to tax "loopholes." A "loophole [assumes] all of

---

[64]James M. Buchanan and Gordon Tullock, *The Calculus of Consent: Logical Foundations of Constitutional Democracy* (Ann Arbor: University of Michigan Press, 1962).

[65]*Logic of Action II*, pp. 269–74.

[66]*Logic of Action I*, p. 252.

everyone's income really belongs to the government."[67] People are accused of using trickery to evade payment, when they in fact are attempting to defend what belongs to them. And in a comment of considerable contemporary relevance, Rothbard notes: "[T]he flat tax would impose an enormous amount of harm and damage to every American homeowner."[68]

In the course of the volume, Rothbard continues his pursuit of a revolutionary question: People have usually looked at an issue in a certain way, but why should we do so?

Thus, an influential approach to welfare economics endeavors to minimize transaction costs. In "The Myth of Neutral Taxation" (1981), Rothbard is ready with an iconoclastic query:

> What is so terrible about transaction costs? On what basis are they considered the ultimate evil, so that their minimization must override all other considerations of choice, freedom, and justice?[69]

If one responds that reducing these costs has some, but not overriding importance, Rothbard's question compels one to specify exactly how much, and why, they are to count.

Fortunately for our society, support among economists for the free market is widespread. For almost any government activity, one can find an economist to argue that the market will provide the service in a better fashion. Yet who but Rothbard would think to ask, why should the government be allowed to collect information?

He makes a simple but devastating point: absent statistical data, the government could not interfere with the economy:

> [S]tatistics are, in a crucial sense, critical to all interventionist and socialistic activities of government. . . . Statistics are the eyes and ears of the bureaucrat, the politician, the socialistic reformer. Only by statistics can they know, or at least have

---

[67] *Logic of Action II*, p. 116.

[68] Ibid., p. 110.

[69] Ibid., p. 88.

any idea about, what is going on in the economy. . . . Cut off those eyes and ears, destroy those crucial guidelines to knowledge, and the whole threat of government intervention is almost completely eliminated.[70]

Perhaps the clearest proof of Rothbard's analytical acumen occurs in an essay on Joseph Schumpeter. As is well known, Schumpeter had a peculiar conception of the entrepreneur. He viewed the great entrepreneurs as virtual forces of nature, exempt from explanation by science. Rothbard shows how Schumpeter's economics forced him to this view. He "den[ied] the role of time in production altogether"[71] and operated with static equations. There was no room for innovation in his unchanging Walrasian prison house: he could deal with radical change only by a total exit from his system. Though a firm defender of deductive method, Rothbard knew very well that a theory must be true to the facts; and his brilliant analysis of the way Schumpeter's conceptual toolkit led him astray is a classic contribution to the history of economics.

Rothbard views deconstructionism with little favor. Deconstructionists claim that texts lack a fixed meaning: the apparent meaning of a text is always accompanied by countervailing patterns. A reader must then "deconstruct" a text rather than take it to have coherent sense. Rothbard raises the key point: why bother? "If we cannot understand the meaning of any texts, then why are we bothering with trying to understand or to take seriously the works or doctrines of authors who aggressively proclaim their own incomprehensibility?"[72]

---

[70]Ibid., pp. 182–83.

[71]Ibid., p. 230.

[72]Ibid., p. 277.

ROTHBARD ON MONEY:
THE VINDICATION OF GOLD

Rothbard devoted close attention to monetary theory. Here he emphasized the virtues of the classical gold standard and supported 100 percent reserve banking. This system, he held, would prevent the credit expansion that, according to the Austrian theory of the business cycle developed by Mises and Friedrich Hayek, led to inevitable depression. His views on money feature prominently in *Man, Economy, and State*. He summarized his ideas for the general public in the often-reprinted pamphlet *What Has Government Done to Our Money?* (1963)[73] and also wrote a textbook, *The Mystery of Banking* (1983);[74] several of the essays in *Making Economic Sense* also discuss monetary policy.[75] His *The Case Against the Fed* (1994)[76] is another popular exposition of his views. His most important theoretical essays on the subject are contained in the first volume of *The Logic of Action*.

He explains with crystal clarity the essentials of Mises's account of money. Monetary theory, for Mises and the Austrians, does not stand isolated from the rest of economics. Through the use of the regression theorem, Mises (following Menger) showed how money develops from barter. Money is properly a commodity, whose value, like that of any other commodity, is determined by the market. Some commodities are much easier to market than others, and "[o]nce any particular commodity starts to be used as a medium,

---

[73]*What Has Government Done to Our Money?* (Colorado Springs, Colo.: Pine Tree Press, 1963).

[74]*The Mystery of Banking* (New York: Richardson and Snyder, 1983).

[75]*Making Economic Sense* (Auburn, Ala.: Ludwig von Mises Institute, 1995).

[76]*The Case Against the Fed* (Auburn, Ala.: Ludwig von Mises Institute, 1994).

this very process has a spiraling, or snowballing, effect."[77] Soon one or two commodities emerge into general use as a medium of exchange. And this, precisely, is money. Gold and silver have almost always been the commodities that win the competition for marketability. "Accordingly, every modern currency unit originated as *a unit of weight of gold or silver*."[78]

This process was no accident; according to the regression theorem, money could not have originated by government fiat. There would be no means to determine the purchasing power of money that was not initially a commodity.

> One of the important achievements of the regression theory is its establishment of the fact that money *must* . . . develop out of a commodity already in demand for direct use, the commodity then being used as a more and more general medium of exchange. Demand for a good as a medium of exchange *must* be predicated on a previously existing array of prices in terms of other goods.[79]

We can already respond to the following question: what is the optimum quantity of money? If one has understood the explanation of money's genesis, the answer is apparent. An increase in the supply of money does not increase real wealth, since money is used only in exchange.[80] "*Any* quantity of money in society is 'optimal'."[81] The answer remains the same when paper money has been introduced.

A problem now arises for the analysis so far presented. If an increase in the supply of money does not increase real wealth, why have governments continually resorted to inflation? Rothbard's

---

[77]Ibid., p. 13.

[78]Ibid., p. 17; emphasis in the original.

[79]*Man, Economy, and State with Power and Market*, pp. 274–75.

[80]The exception of nonmonetary uses of gold and silver can for our purposes be ignored.

[81]*Case Against the Fed*, p. 20; emphasis in the original.

response involves another fundamental insight of Austrian economics. Inflation does not affect everyone equally: quite the contrary, those who first obtain new money gain a great advantage, since they can purchase goods and services before most people become aware that the purchasing power of money has fallen. Politicians use inflation to benefit themselves and their supporters.

Another dubious monetary practice arose out of deposit banking. Because of the inconvenience of carrying gold and silver, people often deposited their money in banks, obtaining in return a receipt. These receipts, since they are promises to pay gold and silver, soon began to circulate as money substitutes. But a temptation presented itself to the bankers. The receipts normally did not specify particular gold or silver coins to be returned to the depositor; they were rather entitlements to specified amounts of the money commodity.[82] Since they are required only to return the amount of money specified in the receipt, bankers might give out more receipts than they had gold and silver on hand, trusting that not all depositors would demand redemption at the same time. For those willing to assume this risk, the prospect of vast profits called appealingly.

But is not this practice a blatant instance of fraud? So it would appear, and so Rothbard firmly avers that it is. Unfortunately, several British legal decisions held otherwise, and the American courts adopted these verdicts as well.

Our banker-counterfeiter, one might assume, can now proceed happily on his way to illicit fortune. But an obstacle confronts him: if he issues more receipts than he can redeem, the clients of other banks might ruin him through demands for payment that he cannot make good. Hence the bankers worked to establish a central banking system. Under a centralized system, the danger of bank runs would diminish. If Rothbard is correct, the entire basis of modern deposit banking, the fractional reserve system, is a type of counterfeiting that must be abolished. Under present arrangements, "the

---

[82]Rothbard noted that the great nineteenth-century economist William Stanley Jevons warned against these "general deposit warrants."

Fed has the well-nigh absolute power to determine the money supply if it so wishes."[83] In response, the Federal Reserve System must be liquidated and the gold standard restored "at one stroke."[84]

In the course of his exposition, Rothbard states: "The Austrian theory of money virtually begins and ends with Mises's monumental *Theory of Money and Credit*,[85] published in 1912."[86] Here Rothbard underestimates himself. He made major advances in monetary theory. In particular, he favored a broader definition than customary of the supply of money—money includes whatever is redeemable at par in standard money.

Rothbard's insistence on conceptual precision contrasts with the pragmatic, "anything goes" position of the Chicago School. In "Austrian Definitions of the Supply of Money" (1978), he castigates that group's "desire to avoid essentialist concepts."[87] Unconcerned with what money is in itself, to the Chicagoites an aridly scholastic question, they call money whatever most closely correlates with national income. Such unconcern with clarity makes Rothbard recoil in horror.

As always with Rothbard, his pursuit of clarity in theory remains closely tied to practice. Given a correct account of theory, various suggestions for monetary reform can at once be seen to be fallacious. Thus, in "The Case for a Genuine Gold Dollar" (1985),[88] Rothbard objects to Hayek's call for denationalization of money. Hayek's call for a multitude of privately issued monies ignores the implications of the regression theorem. Owing to the advantages of a common medium of exchange, barter leads to money; Hayek's proposal would reverse that evolution.

---

[83] *The Case Against the Fed*, p. 144.

[84] Ibid., p. 146.

[85] *Logic of Action I*, p. 297.

[86] Ludwig von Mises, *The Theory of Money and Credit* (Indianapolis: Libery*Classics*, 1980).

[87] *Logic of Action I*, p. 337.

[88] Ibid., pp. 364–83.

Rothbard demolishes freely fluctuating exchange rates with a simple conceptual point. As he notes in "Gold vs. Fluctuating Fiat Exchange Rates" (1975),[89] a "free market for money,"[90] as proposed by Milton Friedman, is on a correct account of money senseless. Money, in the Austrian view, is a commodity: a specific amount of money, then, is a quantity of a commodity, usually (as names such as "pound" suggest) measured by weight. The content of the monetary unit is no more a matter for negotiation on the market than is, say, the length of a foot.

To Rothbard, Keynesian economics was responsible for much of what was wrong with contemporary monetary policy, and he often does battle with it. Lord Keynes and his disciples spurned the gold standard, which Rothbard sees as the only basis for a sound currency. Instead, the Keynesians endeavored to establish a worldwide fiat currency, under the control of an international bank. To achieve this, the Keynesians thought, would eliminate a principal obstacle to their economic plans.

As everyone knows, the Keynesian system often prescribes inflation. But if one country inflates and others do not, or do so only to a lesser extent, it will, under a gold standard, lose gold to them. A Keynesian World Bank would permit all countries to inflate together: gone would be the check that independent monetary systems would impose on radical Keynesianism.

Of course, there is the minor matter that a world Keynesian monetary system spells disaster. "At the end of the road would be a horrendous world-wide hyper-inflation, with no way of escaping into sounder or less inflated currencies."[91] Fortunately, Keynesians have been unable to put their schemes into full operation: but the manifest failure of their system has not deterred them, and they must ever be combated anew. Rothbard's unique combination of political and economic analysis is an indispensable weapon in the struggle.

---

[89]Ibid., pp. 350–63.

[90]Ibid., p. 389

[91]*Making Economic Sense*, p. 254.

But if Keynesianism leads to disaster, wherein lies salvation? One false step, appealing to many, is to cast away theory altogether. The National Bureau of Economic Research has famously attempted to study the business cycle through strict reliance on fact; and Rothbard's teacher Arthur Burns, long associated with the National Bureau, was a partisan of this approach. The Bureau's "proclaimed methodology is Baconian: that is, it trumpets the claim that it *has no* theories, that it collects myriads of facts and statistics, and that its cautiously worded conclusions arise slowly, Phoenix-like, out of the data themselves."[92]

Rothbard subjects the alleged scientific approach of the Bureau to devastating attack. Rothbard, although of course firmly committed to Austrian economics, had a detailed knowledge of statistics, at one time his college major; and he could meet the measurement devotees on their own ground.

AUSTRIAN ECONOMIC HISTORY

Rothbard showed the illumination that Austrian theory could bring to economic history in *America's Great Depression* (1963).[93] Far from being a proof of the failures of unregulated capitalism, the 1929 Depression illustrates rather the dangers of government interference with the economy. The economic collapse came as a necessary correction to the artificial boom induced by the Federal Reserve System's monetary expansion during the 1920s. The attempts by the government to "cure" the downturn served only to make matters worse.

---

[92]Ibid., p. 232.

[93]*America's Great Depression*, 5th ed. (1963; Auburn, Ala.: Ludwig von Mises Institute, 2000).

In arriving at his interpretation, an earlier work influenced him. He considered Lionel Robbins's *The Great Depression*[94] to be "one of the great economic works of our time. . . . This is unquestionably the best work published on the Great Depression."[95] In this evaluation, he differed from Robbins himself, who under the influence of Keynes repudiated his own book.

Robbins adumbrated a theme that Rothbard carried much further in his own book:

> We see how bank credit expansion in the U.S. . . . generated by a desire to inflate in order to help Britain as well as an absurd devotion to a stable price level, drove the civilized world into a great depression. . . . He [Robbins] shows that the U.S. inflation in 1927 and 1928 when it was *losing* gold . . . was in flagrant violation of the "rules" of the gold standard.[96]

Robbins also prefigured a key point in Rothbard's analysis of why the Depression lasted so long.

> Robbins shows how the various nations took measures to counteract and cushion the depression that could only make it worse . . . [e.g.,] keeping up wage rates (e.g., Hoover and his White House conferences)."[97]

But all these basic Austrian points were carried to a new level of precision and depth in *America's Great Depression*.

Rothbard began his work with a presentation of the Austrian theory of the business cycle. The key problem, he says, is

---

[94]Lional Robbins, *The Great Depression* (London: Macmillan, 1934).
[95]Letter to Ivan Bierly, November 14, 1959; Rothbard Papers.
[96]Ibid.
[97]Ibid.

> *why is there a sudden general cluster of business errors?* . . . Business activity moves along nicely with most business firms making handsome profits. Suddenly, without warning, conditions change and the bulk of business firms are experiencing losses; they are suddenly revealed to have made grievous errors in forecasting.[98]

A good theory must also explain why, over the course of the cycle, capital goods industries fluctuate more than do consumer goods industries. A third requirement is that it account for the increase in the quantity of money during the boom.

The Austrian theory permits us to account for all three of these conditions. The rate of interest is determined by the rate of time preference, i.e., the preference people have for present goods over future goods. The balance between consumers' goods and capital goods depends on this rate. With a low rate of time preference, more investment in the "higher" stages of production will occur; if, however, people shift to preferring more immediate satisfaction, the structure of production will adjust accordingly. Investment will shift from capital goods to consumers' goods industries.

So far, so good; but an infusion of bank credit can upset matters. The extra credit depresses the rate of interest below the "natural" rate, i.e., the rate in accord with peoples' rate of time preference. With money available for loans at lower interest rates than before, projects in the higher stages that could not previously be undertaken become profitable.

> Businessmen, in short, are misled by the bank inflation into believing that the supply of funds is greater than it really is . . . . Businessmen take their newly acquired funds and bid up the prices of capital and other producers' goods, and this stimulates a shift of investment from the "lower" (near the consumer) to the "higher" orders of production (furthest away from the consumer)—from consumer goods to capital goods industries.[99]

---

[98]*America's Great Depression*, p. 8.

[99]Ibid., pp. 10–11.

When the bank credit expansion ends, the money rate of interest rises to the natural rate; there is in general no reason to assume that the expansion has changed the rate of time preference. The rise in the interest rate now makes the expanded investments in the higher stages unprofitable. Consumers' preferences require a shift from capital goods to consumer goods industries. The shift, i.e., the liquidation of the capital goods expansion, is precisely the depression.

In the Austrian view, the depression is the necessary phase of adjustment; the government must not try to maintain the level of spending, as this will serve only to prolong the process by which the economy achieves the balance between consumers and capital goods industries that consumers want.

Rothbard contrasts the Austrian theory of the cycle with competing accounts. Joseph Schumpeter's "cycle theory is notable for being the only doctrine, apart from the Austrian, to be grounded on, and integrated with, general economic theory."[100] In Schumpeter's view, bank credit expansion also plays a crucial role. But here the mechanism differs from that in the Austrian theory. Schumpeter maintains that the credit expansion finances a cluster of innovations. When innovations decline, a depression ensues.

Rothbard finds this account unsatisfactory.

> The theory postulates a periodic cluster of innovations in the boom periods. But there is no reasoning advanced to account for such an odd cluster. On the contrary, innovations, technological advance, take place continually, and in most, not just a few, firms.[101]

Having dispatched Schumpeter's account, as well as numerous others, Rothbard applies Austrian theory to the concrete events of the 1920s and early 1930s. As expected, he argues that during the 1920s, an inflationary boom occurred. To grasp his point clearly, it is essential to bear in mind what he means by "inflation." He does

---

[100]Ibid., pp. 72–73.
[101]Ibid., p. 74.

not mean an increase in the level of prices. Rather, "inflation is not precisely the increase in total money supply; it is the increase in money supply *not consisting in*, i.e., not covered by, an increase in gold, the standard commodity money."[102]

Given this view, Chicago School criticisms of Rothbard that stress price level stability miss the mark. Rothbard is interested in the amount of bank credit expansion, which on the Austrian view generates the boom. The Chicago School monetarists, by contrast,

> uphold as an ethical and economic ideal the maintenance of a stable, constant price level. The essence of the cycle is supposed to be the rise and fall—the movements—of the price level. Since this level is determined by monetary forces, the monetarists hold that if the price level is kept constant by government policy, the business cycle will disappear. [Milton] Friedman . . . emulates his mentors in lauding Benjamin Strong for keeping the wholesale price level stable during the 1920s. To the monetarists, the inflation of money and bank credit engineered by Strong led to no ill effects, no cycle of boom and bust; on the contrary, the Great Depression was caused by the tight money policy that ensued after Strong's death.[103]

Ironically, in Rothbard's historical account, the attempt by the Federal Reserve to maintain stable prices in part led to the inflationary bank credit expansion that caused the cycle. The Chicago cure is the Austrian disease. Rothbard documents in great detail the popularity of the stable price theory among American economists, with Irving Fisher leading the way.

> The siren song of a stable price level had lured leading politicians, to say nothing of economists, as early as 1911. It was then that Professor Irving Fisher launched his career as head of the "stable money" movement in the United States.[104]

---

[102]Ibid., p. 94.

[103]Ibid., p. xxxiii.

[104]Ibid., p. 174.

Rothbard describes in careful detail the motives and policies of the Federal Reserve during the 1920s, stressing the cooperation between Benjamin Strong and "the Mephistopheles of the inflation of the 1920s," Montagu Norman of the Bank of England.[105] His verdict is severe:

> We may conclude that the Federal Reserve authorities, in promulgating their inflationary policies, were motivated not only by the desire to help British inflation and to subsidize farmers, but were also guided—or rather misguided—by the fashionable economic theory of a stable price level as the goal of monetary manipulation.[106]

When disaster struck in October 1929, many economists, still under the delusion of price stability, urged increased government spending; and Rothbard devotes much attention to their views and activities. Unfortunately, President Hoover enthusiastically embraced their views. Although Hoover

> was only a moderate inflationist relative to many others. . . . Seeing money-in-circulation increase by $800 million in 1931, Hoover engineered a coordinated hue-and-cry against "traitorous hoarding." "Hoarding," of course, meant that individuals were choosing to redeem their own property, to ask banks to transform their deposits into the cash which the banks had promised to have on hand for redemption.[107]

Worst of all, Hoover's constant efforts to prop up wages helped prolong mass unemployment.

> Hoover had prevented "an immediate attack upon wages as a basis of maintaining profits," but the result of wiping out profits and maintaining artificial wage rates was chronic, unprecedented depression.[108]

---

[105]Ibid., p. 154.
[106]Ibid., p. 181.
[107]Ibid., p. 306.
[108]Ibid., p. 322.

In making this argument, Rothbard became a pioneer in "Hoover revisionism." Contrary to the myths promoted by Hoover himself and his acolytes, Hoover was not an opponent of big government. Quite the contrary, the economic policies of the "Engineer in Politics" prefigured the New Deal, although he did not go to the lengths of his successor. "Yet, if New Deal socialism was the logic of Hoover's policy, he cautiously extended the logic only so far."[109] Rothbard's view of Hoover is now widely accepted. Joan Hoff Wilson's *Herbert Hoover: Forgotten Progressive*, is important in this connection.[110]

Rothbard displayed little patience for historians who perpetuated the old myths about Hoover. In a review of *The Hoover Leadership*[111] by Edgar Eugene Robinson, a Hoover stalwart, Rothbard remarks:

> There is also the usual Hooverite complaining at FDR's lack of "cooperation" in the Interregnum, and blaming the remainder of the depression on that; actually, it is rarely pointed out that the "cooperation" would have meant cooperation in New Deal inflationist measures . . . Robinson . . . virtually ignores any alternatives or criticism of the Hoover policies, except the extreme New Deal or socialist one.[112]

It is safe to say that Rothbard would have viewed another book with much more favor. In his *A History of the American People*,[113] the world-renowned journalist and popular historian Paul Johnson adopts a thoroughly Rothbardian account of the onset of the 1929

---

[109]Ibid., p. 323.

[110]Joan Hoff Wilson, *Herbert Hoover: Forgotten Progressive* (New York: Little Brown, 1975).

[111]Edgar Eugene Robinson, *The Hoover Leadership, 1933–1945* (New York: Lippincott, 1955).

[112]Letter to Kenneth Templeton, August 19, 1961; Rothbard Papers.

[113]Paul Johnson, *A History of the American People* (New York: Harper Collins, 1997).

Depression. Like Rothbard, he finds the source of the collapse in irresponsible credit expansion: "[D]uring the 1920s the United States, in conjunction with British and other leading industrial and financial powers, tried to keep the world prosperous by deliberately inflating the money supply."[114]

The currency expansion owed much to the influence of John Maynard Keynes:

> In fact Keynes's *Tract (on Monetary Reform)* advocating "managed currency" and a stabilized price-level, both involving constant government interference, coordinated internationally, was part of the problem.[115]

The market crash of 1929 "ought to have been welcome. . . . Business downturns serve essential purposes. They have to be sharp. But they need not be long because they are self-adjusting."[116] Unfortunately, Herbert Hoover did not realize this essential truth. Far from being a supporter of laissez-faire, he was an ardent interventionist whose policies impeded recovery. "Hoover was a social engineer. Roosevelt was a social psychologist. But neither understood the Depression, or how to cure it."[117] The Rothbardian influence is evident, and Johnson scrupulously cites Rothbard's works several times.[118]

In his Introduction to the fifth edition of *America's Great Depression*, Johnson makes clear his admiration: "His book is an intellectual *tour de force*, in that it consists, from start to finish, of a sustained thesis, presented with relentless logic, abundant illustration, and great eloquence."[119]

---

[114]Ibid., p. 727.

[115]Ibid., p. 729.

[116]Ibid., pp. 734–35.

[117]Ibid., p. 736.

[118]Ibid., pp. 733–35.

[119]Quoted in *America's Great Depression*, pp. xv–xvi.

For Rothbard, banking policy was a key not only to the Great Depression but to the whole of American economic history. Like Michelet, he believed that history is a resurrection of the flesh; and his discussions are no dry-as-dust presentations of statistics. He was always concerned to identify the particular actors and interests behind historical decisions. The struggle between the competing Morgan and Rockefeller banking circles figures again and again in his articles in this field, collected in his *A History of Money and Banking in the United States* (1999).[120]

In this book, he displays to the full his remarkable ability to throw unexpected light on historical controversies. Throughout his work, he pointed out factors that earlier authors had over-looked.

An example will illustrate Rothbard's technique. Everyone knows Lenin's theory of imperialism. Developed capitalist economies, Lenin maintained, characteristically produce more than they can sell domestically. To find an outlet for their surplus goods, capitalists seek markets abroad. Their endeavors bring about a struggle for colonies; the "highest stage" of capitalism is imperialism.

So much is well known; but how did Lenin arrive at this view? The standard accounts point to J.A. Hobson; earlier, Marx himself had suggested a version of the theory. He, in turn, was influenced by Edward Gibbon Wakefield. But Rothbard has unearthed another, and most surprising, source: capitalist supporters of imperialism.

> By the late 1890s, groups of theoreticians in the United States were working on what would later be called the "Leninist'" theory of capitalist imperialism. The theory was originated, not by Lenin but by advocates of imperialism, centering around such Morgan-oriented friends and brain trusts of Theodore Roosevelt as Henry Adams, Brooks

---

[120]*A History of Money and Banking in the United States: The Colonial Era to World War II* (Auburn, Ala.: Ludwig von Mises Institute, 2002).

> Adams, Admiral Alfred T. Mahan, and Massachusetts Senator
> Henry Cabot Lodge. . . . The ever lower rate of profit from
> the "surplus capital" was in danger of crippling capitalism,
> except that salvation loomed in the form of foreign markets
> and especially foreign investments. . . . Hence, to save
> advanced capitalism, it was necessary for Western govern-
> ments to engage in outright imperialist or neo-imperialist
> ventures, which would force other countries to open their
> markets for American products and would force open invest-
> ment opportunities abroad.[121]

He does not confine himself to a general statement of the
monopoly capitalist origins of the Leninist theory. He describes in
great detail the activities of Charles Conant, a leading advocate of
imperialism. Conant, it transpires, did much more than theorize.
He actively worked to install the gold-exchange standard, a key
tool of American monetary imperialism, in Latin America and
elsewhere. Rothbard describes Conant's activities in his unique
style: "Conant, as usual, was the major theoretician and fina-
gler."[122]

Neither as theorist nor practitioner did Conant act on his own,
and to see why not enables us to grasp a central plank of Rothbard's
edifice.

> Nor should it be thought that Charles A. Conant was the
> purely disinterested scientist he claimed to be. His currency
> reforms directly benefited his investment banker employers.
> Thus, Conant was treasurer, from 1902 to 1906, of the Mor-
> gan-run Morton Trust Company of New York, and it was
> surely no coincidence that Morton Trust was the bank that
> held the reserve funds for the governments of the Philip-
> pines, Panama, and the Dominican Republic, after their
> respective currency reforms.[123]

---

[121]Ibid., pp. 209–10.

[122]Ibid., p. 226.

[123]Ibid., pp. 232–33.

Rothbard maintained that the House of Morgan held effective control of the American government for much of the late nineteenth and early twentieth centuries, down to the onset of Franklin Roosevelt's New Deal in 1933. He traces in detail Morgan backing for a central bank, culminating in the creation of the Federal Reserve System in 1913. His *Wall Street, Banks, and American Foreign Policy*[124] and *The Case Against the Fed* are other presentations of his thesis.

The House of Morgan was by no means the first group in American history to seek the ill-gotten gains of centralized banking. Rothbard discusses in great detail, e.g., the struggles over the First and Second Banks of the United States.

The Federal Reserve System, Rothbard makes clear, was the culmination of efforts that continued throughout the nineteenth century to centralize banking.

> By the 1890s, the leading Wall Street bankers were becoming increasingly disgruntled with their own creation, the National Banking System . . . while the banking system was partially centralized under their leadership, it was not centralized *enough*.[125]

As he describes the movement to cartelize banking, Rothbard introduces a dominant theme in his interpretation of twentieth-century American history: the struggle of competing groups of bankers for power.

> From the 1890s until World War II, much of American political history . . . can be interpreted not so much as "Democrat" versus "Republican," but as the interaction or conflict between the Morgans and their allies on the one hand, and the Rockefeller-Harriman-Kuhn, Loeb alliance on the other.[126]

---

[124]*Wall Street, Banks, and American Foreign Policy* (1984; Burlingame, Calif.: Center for Libertarian Studies, 1995).

[125]*Case Against the Fed*, p. 79; emphasis in the original.

[126]Ibid. p. 92.

In the agitation to establish a central bank, the House of Morgan was in the ascendant; and Rothbard stresses the importance of the conference held at Jekyll Island, Georgia, under Morgan control, in planning for the Federal Reserve System.

Throughout his narrative, Rothbard stresses a point vital to the understanding of monetary history. A popular belief holds that poor people, likely to be in debt, favor easy money, while their rich creditors oppose it.

Often, this turns out to be the reverse of the truth.

> Debtors benefit from inflation and creditors lose; realizing this fact, older historians assumed that debtors were largely poor agrarians and creditors were wealthy merchants and that therefore the former were the main sponsors of inflationary nostrums. But, of course, there are no rigid "classes" of creditors and debtors; indeed, wealthy merchants and land speculators are often the heaviest debtors.[127]

Here Rothbard continued the work of his mentor Joseph Dorfman.

> Dorfman, in the mid-1940s, arrived at the conclusion that the Beardian class-struggle thesis—the old debtor vs. creditor, East-West, farmer-merchant, interpretation of all the struggles of American economic policy (e.g., over cheap money) was complete nonsense. . . . Dorfman's thesis was that on each side of every economic dispute were merchants, respectable men, farmers, etc.[128]

Investment bankers profit by encouraging debt. Rothbard maintains that investment bankers are especially likely to form alliances with the government; hence their activities must be viewed with the greatest suspicion.

------

[127]*A History of Money and Banking in the United States*, p. 58.
[128]Letter to Ivan Bierly, November 14, 1959; Rothbard Papers.

Investment bankers do much of their business underwriting government bonds, in the United States and abroad. Therefore, they have a vested interest in promoting deficits and in forcing taxpayers to redeem government debt. Both sets of bankers [i.e., commercial and investment], then, tend to be tied in with government policy, and try to influence and control government actions in domestic and foreign affairs.[129]

He applies this thesis to interpret American foreign policy:

The great turning point of American foreign policy came in the early 1890s, during the second Cleveland Administration. It was then that the U.S. turned sharply and permanently from a foreign policy of peace and non-intervention to an aggressive program of economic and political expansion abroad.[130]

The turn came at the behest of the House of Morgan, which had already obtained the controlling influence on American foreign policy it was to retain until the onset of the New Deal.

Under the new activist policy, the United States vigorously sought to wrest control of the Latin American market from Great Britain. In spite of the later partnership between the Morgan interests and Britain, the United States was very far indeed from alliance with Britain during most of the 1890s.

But a British-American partnership was not long in coming, and Rothbard finds in the close ties between the House of Morgan and British financial interests an underlying cause of American entry into World War I. Because of Morgan investments in allied war bonds and in the export of war munitions, "J.P. Morgan and his associates did everything they possibly could to push the supposedly neutral United States into the war on the side of England

---

[129]*Wall Street, Banks, and American Foreign Policy*, p. 1.

[130]Ibid., p. 4.

and France."[131] Further, "Benjamin Strong obligingly doubled the money supply to finance America's role in the war effort."[132]

Rothbard's last point serves to introduce a story within the larger story of Morgan influence. Benjamin Strong, the Governor of the New York Federal Reserve Bank, was by far the most influential figure in the entire Federal Reserve System from its inception until his death in 1928. He entered into close association with Montagu Norman, Governor of the Bank of England. Both men had enlisted in the Morgan camp.

> While the close personal relations between Strong and Norman were of course highly important for the collaboration that formed the international monetary world of the 1920s, it should not be overlooked that both were intimately bound to the House of Morgan.[133]

At Norman's behest, Strong during the 1920s inflated the U.S. monetary supply, in order to enable Britain to maintain in operation the gold-exchange standard. By doing so, Rothbard claims, Strong bears heavy responsibility for the onset of the 1929 stock market crash and the ensuing depression.

> The United States inflated its money and credit in order to prevent inflationary Britain from losing gold to the United States, a loss which would endanger the new, jerry-built "gold standard" structure. The result, however, was eventual collapse of money and credit in the U.S. and abroad, and a worldwide depression. Benjamin Strong was the Morgans' architect of a disastrous policy of inflationary boom that led inevitably to bust.[134]

---

[131]Ibid., p. 16.
[132]*A History of Money and Banking in the United States*, p. 270.
[133]Ibid., p. 374.
[134]Ibid., p. 271.

The book's narrative is a complex one, and it by no means reduces to an account of the vicissitudes of the House of Morgan. A rival banking group, consisting most importantly of Rockefeller interests, challenged it for supremacy. For Rothbard, the New Deal can best be viewed as the victory of the Rockefeller group; he cites in this connection the political scientist Thomas Ferguson. Although the Morgans recovered some of their influence after the mid-1930s, they henceforward occupied a subordinate position.

Throughout the book, Rothbard pursues with tenacity a biographical method of analysis that stresses the ties of influential figures to central financial groups, such as the Morgans. In his intricate tracing of patrons and clients, Rothbard brings to mind the great works of Ronald Syme and Lewis Namier. But Rothbard has the advantage over these renowned historians in that he does not restrict himself to the amassing of biographical detail. He has in addition a carefully worked out theory, Austrian economics, to guide him.

A ROTHBARDIAN VIEW OF AMERICAN HISTORY

Rothbard ranged far beyond economics in his historical work. In a four-volume series, *Conceived in Liberty*, (1975–1979)[135] he presented a detailed account of American colonial history that stressed the libertarian antecedents of the American Revolution. His fundamental thesis emerges in his discussion of seventeenth-century developments. He states:

---

[135] *Conceived in Liberty*, vol. I: *A New Land, A New People: The American Colonies in the Seventeenth Century*; vol. II: *"Salutary Neglect": The American Colonies in the First Half of the Eighteenth Century*; vol. III: *Advance to Revolution, 1760–1775*; vol. IV: *The Revolutionary War, 1775–1784* (1979; Auburn, Ala.: Ludwig von Mises Institute, 1999).

> The noted historian Carl Becker once raised the question
> about the extent to which the American Revolution was a bat-
> tle for "home rule" of the colonies *vis-à-vis* England, as
> opposed to a battle of "who should rule at home," within the
> colonies. . . . We are now able to frame a judgment about this
> issue for the earlier revolutions of the late seventeenth cen-
> tury and for their aftermath. We have seen how revolution, in
> the 1670s and especially after 1688, swept almost every
> colony in America: from Bacon's Rebellion in Virginia to
> Leisler's in New York to the continuing state of revolution in
> the two New Jerseys. All of these revolutions may be classi-
> fied as "liberal" and popular; in short, as essentially mass
> movements in behalf of libertarian objectives and in opposi-
> tion to the tyranny, high taxes, monopolies, and restrictions
> imposed by the various governments.[136]

Because the revolts were directed against state oppression, the
antithesis of internal versus external revolution posed by Becker
must be rejected:

> [W]hen these colonies rebelled, they did so not against Eng-
> land *per se*, but against the oppressions of the state, domi-
> nated by the English government. And the fact that the sud-
> den weakening of English authority during the Glorious Rev-
> olution touched off these revolts in no sense negates this con-
> clusion.[137]

The Colonial Era, in Rothbard's view, was not entirely a battle
for liberty. He had little use for New England Puritanism:

> One basic influence on colonial American thought was the
> fact that two contrasting traditions emerged from its Protes-
> tant and Puritan heritage. One was the fanatical theocratic
> persecuting tradition, which reached its apogee in Massachu-
> setts Bay and the Dutch Orange Party.[138]

---

[136]*Conceived in Liberty*, vol. I, p. 510.
[137]Ibid.
[138]Ibid., vol. II, p. 188.

His grim judgment in part rests on the detailed account in the preceding volume of the persecution of the antinomian Anne Hutchinson. He recommends Thomas Jefferson Wertenbaker's *The Puritan Oligarchy*[139] as "brilliant and deeply critical."[140]

Much more to Rothbard's liking was the other tradition:

> The other was optimistic, individualist, libertarian, and even deistic, and was reflected in the Levellers, and in such escapees from Massachusetts as Anne Hutchinson and Roger Williams, and later in Charles Chauncy and Jonathan Mayhew.[141]

He stresses the influence of "Algernon Sidney, John Locke, and Trenchard and Gordon of *Cato's Letters*. Each made a profound contribution to the growth and development of libertarian thought in America."[142]

He views Locke as in essence a radical libertarian:

> There were two strains in Locke's *Essay*: the individualist and libertarian, and the conservative and majoritarian, and examples of caution and inconsistency are easy to find. But the individualist view is the core of the argument. . . . Locke was an extraordinarily secretive and timorous writer on political affairs. . . . Hence it is not unreasonable to assume that the conservative strain in Locke was a camouflage for the radically libertarian core of his position.[143]

---

[139]Thomas Jefferson Wertenbaker, *The Puritan Oligarchy* (New York: Charles Scribner's Sons, 1947).

[140]*Conceived in Liberty*, vol. I, p. 516.

[141]Ibid., vol. II, p. 188.

[142]Ibid.

[143]Ibid., p. 190. Willmoore Kendall, whom we shall soon encounter, interpreted Locke as a majoritarian; Rothbard's criticism of Kendall can be seen as a radical Lockean assault on a conservative Lockean.

Trenchard and Gordon interpreted Locke in just this way; they "greatly radicalized the impact of Locke's libertarian creed."[144] *Cato's Letters*[145] warned against the tyranny of power. This constantly threatened liberty and must, if necessary, be checked by revolution.

> "Cato" assured his readers that there was no danger that the public might exercise its right of revolution against tyrannical government too frequently or imprudently; due to settled habits, as well as the propaganda and power of government, the danger is quite the reverse.[146]

Rothbard's comments here raise a fundamental issue: how influential are intellectuals such as Locke and Trenchard and Gordon, and what motivates them? His response expresses a fundamental feature of his entire approach to history. He contrasts two sorts of intellectual: "court intellectuals," who serve those in authority, primarily wish to gain money and power for themselves. Revolutionary intellectuals, who oppose the state, do so out of genuine conviction.

He minces no words about the former group:

> The ruling class—be it warlords, nobles, bureaucrats, feudal landlords, monopoly merchants, or a coalition of several of these groups—must employ intellectuals to convince the majority of the public that its rule is beneficent, inevitable, necessary, and even divine. The leading role of the intellectual throughout history is that of the court intellectual, who, in return for a share of, a junior partnership in, the power and pelf offered by the rest of the ruling class, spins the apologias for state rule with which to convince a misguided public.[147]

---

[144]Ibid., p. 192.

[145]John Trenchard and Thomas Gordon, *Cato's Letters, or Essays on Liberty, Civil and Religious, and Other Important Subjects*, 4 vols. (New York: Russell and Russell, 1969).

[146]*Conceived in Liberty*, vol. I, p. 195.

[147]Ibid., vol. III, p. 352.

Rothbard agreed with Étienne de la Boétie and David Hume that government depends on popular support: "no state—no minority—can continue long in power unless supported, even if passively, by the majority."[148] Hence the imperative need for intellectuals to guide the public.

The case is far different for revolutionary intellectuals.

> It is usually directly in the economic interests of the radical intellectuals to allow themselves to "sell out," to be coopted by the ruling state apparatus. The intellectuals who do choose the radical opposition path . . . can scarcely be dominated by economic motives; on the contrary, only a fiercely held ideology, centering on a passion for justice, can keep the intellectuals to the rigorous path of truth. . . .Thus, statists tend to be governed by economic motivation, with ideology serving as a smokescreen for such motives, while libertarians or antistatists are ruled principally and centrally by ideology, with economic defense playing a subordinate role.[149]

When he turns to the American Revolution itself, Rothbard, as usual, challenges mainstream opinion. The virtues and military leadership of George Washington did not impress him.

> Washington set out to transform a people's army, uniquely suited for a libertarian revolution, into another orthodox and despotically ruled statist force after the familiar European model. His primary aim was to crush the individualistic and democratic spirit of the American forces.[150]

For Rothbard, the Articles of Confederation were not, contrary to most historians, an overly weak arrangement that needed to be replaced by the more centrally focused Constitution. Quite the contrary, the Articles themselves allowed too much central control.

---

[148]Ibid.

[149]Ibid., pp. 353–54.

[150]Ibid., vol. IV, p. 43.

> While the radicals had succeeded in pulling much of the cen-
> tralist teeth, the Articles were still a momentous step from
> the loose but effective unity of the original Continental Con-
> gress to the creation of a powerful new central government.
> To that extent, they were an important victory for conser-
> vatism and centralization, and proved to be a half-way house
> on the road to the Constitution.[151]

For Rothbard, this was decidedly the wrong road.

He emphasizes the radical nature of the Revolution.

> It was the first successful war of national liberation against
> western imperialism. A people's war, waged by the majority of
> Americans having the courage and the zeal to rise up against
> constituted "legitimate" government, actually threw off their
> "sovereign."[152]

To this it might be objected that an external revolution need not
be internally radical as well; but Rothbard stands ready with his
answer:

> the sudden smashing of that [British] rule inevitably threw
> government back into a fragmented, local, quasi-anarchistic
> form. When we consider also that the Revolution was con-
> sciously and radically directed against taxes and against cen-
> tral government power, the inevitable thrust of the Revolu-
> tion for a radical transformation toward liberty becomes crys-
> tal clear.[153]

Thomas Jefferson and Tom Paine rank high among the heroes
of this radical drive toward liberty. Paine in *Common Sense*

> not only laid bare the roots of monarchy, but provided a bril-
> liant insight into the nature and origins of the State itself. He
> had made a crucial advance in libertarian theory upon the
> social-contract doctrine of the origin of the State. While he

---

[151]Ibid., p. 254.

[152]Ibid., p. 443.

[153]Ibid., pp. 444–45.

followed Locke in holding that the State *should* be confined to the protection of man's natural rights, he saw clearly that actual states had not originated in this way or for this purpose. Instead, they had been born in naked conquest and plunder.[154]

By contrast, he agrees with Richard Henry Lee that Benjamin Franklin was a "wicked old man."[155]

Rothbard did not address nineteenth century American history in as much detail as the colonial period; but his illuminating article, "Origins of the Welfare State in America" offers a key to his interpretation of this period.[156] He argues that the welfare state cannot be traced to the labor movement. Rather, Yankee postmillennial pietists led the way to statist social reform. They were the product of the Second Great Awakening, led by Charles Finney. Believing that Christ would not return to earth until the world was reformed, they sought to regenerate the social order through state coercion.

> After only a few years of agitation, it was clear to these new Protestants that the Kingdom of God on Earth could only be established by government, which was required to bolster the salvation of individuals by stamping out occasions for sin.[157]

Among the main sins to be combated were drinking ("Demon Rum") and "any activities on the Sabbath except praying and reading the Bible." The postmillennial pietists strongly opposed the Catholic Church; the public school movement in large part was an attempt to "Protestantize" the children of Catholic immigrants.

This group was largely concentrated in New England. "The concentration of the new statists in Yankee areas was nothing short of remarkable."[158] They soon came to embrace big government

---

[154]Ibid., p. 137.

[155]Ibid., p. 360.

[156]*Journal of Libertarian Studies* 12, no. 2 (Fall, 1996): 193–229.

[157]Ibid., p. 199.

[158]Ibid., p. 200.

for the economy as well. "Using big government to create a perfect economy seemed to parallel employing such government to
stamp out sin and create a perfect society."[159] The PMP's [post-
millennial pietists] gravitated to the Republican Party.

"On the other hand, all religious groups that did not want to be
subjected to the PMP theocracy . . . naturally gravitated toward the
laissez-faire political party, the Democrats."[160] Rothbard maintains that the struggle between the PMP's and their Democratic
opponents lay at the heart of the political campaigns of much of
the nineteenth century.

Toward the end of the century, the Progressive intellectuals
often became secularized. Their emphasis shifted

> more and more away from Christ and religion, which became
> ever-vaguer and woollier, and more and more toward a Social
> Gospel, with government correcting, organizing, and eventu-
> ally planning the perfect society.[161]

Richard T. Ely and his student John R. Commons were crucial
figures in this transition. Another was

> the prophet of atheistic higher Democracy, the philosopher
> John Dewey. . . . It is little known that in an early stage of his
> seemingly endless career, Dewey was an ardent preacher of
> postmillennialism and the coming of the Kingdom.[162]

Rothbard also considered the Progressives in his essay "World
War I as Fulfillment: Power and the Intellectuals."[163] He docu-
mented to the hilt that the progressive intellectuals, "advanced

---

[159]Ibid., p. 201.

[160]Ibid., p. 201–02.

[161]Ibid., p. 204.

[162]Ibid., pp. 207–08.

[163]*Journal of Libertarian Studies* 9, no. 1 (Winter, 1984): 81–125.
Reprinted in John V. Denson, ed. *The Costs of War: America's Pyrrhic
Victories*, 2nd ed. (New Brunswick, N.J.: Transaction, 1999).

thinkers," in their own estimation, were quite willing to impose suffering and death upon others, if doing so would advance their mad schemes. As he notes: "War . . . offered a golden opportunity to bring about collectivist social control in the interest of social justice."[164] Once more, John Dewey is a major figure. "Force, he declared, was simply 'a means of getting results' and therefore could neither be lauded nor condemned per se."[165]

THE UNKNOWN ROTHBARD: UNPUBLISHED PAPERS

In his work for the Volker Fund, Rothbard wrote a large number of reports on books and issues. These reports are much more than displays of Rothbard's virtuosity: they frequently offer fuller discussions of vital points in his thought than are available in his books and articles. Unfortunately, they have hitherto remained unpublished. Dr. Roberta Modugno, in a veritable triumph of Rothbardian scholarship, has made available to the public for the first time a selection from the most important of these reports, in Italian translation, in her *Diritto, natura e ragione: Scritti inediti versus Hayek, Mises, Strauss e Polanyi*[166]; most of them, however remain unpublished. It is safe to say that future research on Rothbard will devote much attention to them; here only a few items can be described.

---

[164]Denson, ed., *The Costs of War*, p. 271.

[165]Ibid.

[166]*Diritto, natura e ragione: Scritti inediti versus Hayek, Mises, Strauss e Polanyi*, Roberta Modugno, ed. (Soveria Mannelli, Italy: Rubbettino, 2005). Translated as *Right, Nature, and Reason: Unpublished Writings Versus Hayek, Mises, Strauss and Polanyi*. An English edition is being prepared by the Ludwig von Mises Institute.

Rothbard firmly believed in an objective ethics; and in this stance he found himself in the unfamiliar position of agreement with Leo Strauss. Commenting on Strauss's paper "Relativism," Rothbard writes: "Strauss has one good point, and one alone: that there exists an absolute ethics for man, discoverable by reason, in accordance with [the] natural law of human nature."[167] Rothbard found Strauss effective in his criticism of assorted relativists and historicists:

> Strauss begins [an essay on relativism] with the almost incredibly confused and overrated Isaiah Berlin, and he has no trouble demolishing Berlin and exposing his confusions— Berlin trying to be at the same time an exponent of "positive freedom," "negative freedom," absolutism, and relativism.[168]

Strauss shows that, "in denying the possibility of rational ends [as relativists do] rational means are not on a very secure basis either."[169]

Why should we believe in an objective ethics? Both Rothbard and Strauss found persuasive an appeal to ordinary language. The signature tune of David Hume and his many successors, the "fact-value dichotomy,"[170] is an artificial construction. Suppose, e.g., that someone pushes you aside while you are waiting in line for a movie. Has he not acted rudely? The judgment that he is rude is not a matter for subjective decision but is governed by objective criteria. But surely "rude" is a value-term: what then has happened to the alleged dichotomy between fact and value? In the view favored by Rothbard and Strauss, value judgments are factual. If so, is it not also true—though this is much more controversial— that if human beings need certain things in order to flourish, this

---

[167]"Comments on Relativism Symposium," Rothbard Papers; Modugno, ed, *Diritto, natura e ragione*, p. 137. The quotations are from the original English reports in the Rothbard Papers; page references refer to the Italian translation in Modugno's book.

[168]Ibid., p. 137.

[169]Ibid., p. 138.

[170]*The Ethics of Liberty* (New York: New York University Press), p. 14.

is at once a factual statement and a value judgment? So Rothbard maintained; the influential English philosopher Philippa Foot has also defended this position in her *Natural Goodness*.[171]

Though Rothbard and Strauss were here allied, they soon diverged. Strauss contrasted natural and medieval natural law with "modern" natural law, culminating in the thought of John Locke, to the distinct disadvantage of the latter. As Strauss saw matters, Machiavelli and Hobbes abandoned the classical pursuit of virtue. Instead, they founded political philosophy on passion and self-interest. Locke, despite his professed adherence to natural law, was a secret Hobbesian; he perverted true natural law. Strauss's antipathy to individualism, by the way, should not surprise us. As was often the case, Strauss followed the thought of his much-admired friend, the English socialist historian R.H. Tawney.[172]

Rothbard left no doubt about his view of this interpretation:

> Strauss, while favoring what he considers to be the classical and Christian concepts of natural law, is bitterly opposed to the 17th and 18th century conceptions of Locke and the rationalists, particularly to their "abstract," "deductive," championing of the natural rights of the individual: liberty, property, etc. In this reading, Hobbes and Locke are the great villains in the alleged perversion of natural law. To my mind, this "perversion" was a healthy sharpening and developing of the concept.[173]

Rothbard has the better of the argument, if one takes account of the major study of Brian Tierney, *The Idea of Natural Rights*.[174] As Modugno notes,

---

[171]Philippa Foot, *Natural Goodness* (Oxford University Press, 2001).

[172]See Simon J.D. Green, "The Tawney-Strauss Connection: On Historicism and Values in the History of Political Ideas," *Journal of Modern History* 67 (June 1995): 255–77.

[173]Rothbard Papers; Modugno, ed, *Diritto, natura e ragione*, p. 114.

[174]Brian Tierney, *The Idea of Natural Rights: Studies on Natural Rights, Natural Law, and Church Law 1150–1625* (Atlanta: Scholars Press, 1997).

> Tierney has decisively brought into question the idea of
> Strauss and [Michel] Villey of an antithesis between an
> ancient Aristotelian doctrine of natural law and a modern
> theory of subjective natural rights.[175]

Tierney, one of the world's foremost authorities on medieval canon law, finds numerous uses of the language of individual rights in the writings of twelfth-century Decretists such as Rufinus and the "greatest of them all, Huguccio."[176]

> Many canonists included in their lists of meanings a subjec-
> tive one that explained *ius naturale* as a faculty or power
> inherent in human nature . . . from the beginning, the sub-
> jective idea of natural right was not derived from Christian
> revelation or from some all-embracing natural-law theory of
> cosmic harmony but from an understanding of human nature
> itself as rational, self-aware, and morally responsible.[177]

As all readers of Rothbard know, the key principle of his ethics is the axiom of self-ownership; and this too has medieval antecedents. Tierney finds that "one of the most illustrious masters of the University of Paris in the latter part of the thirteenth century," Henry of Ghent, had a firm grasp of this principle.[178] Henry asked whether a criminal condemned to death had the right to flee and argued that he did: "Only the criminal himself has a property right in his own body or, as Henry put it, 'only the soul under God has property in the substance of the body'."[179]

----

[175]Rothbard Papers; Modugno, ed, *Diritto, natura e ragione*, p. 15.

[176]Tierney, *The Idea of Natural Rights*, p. 64. The Decretists were commentators on the major compilation of canon law, the *Decretum Gratiani*.

[177]Ibid., p. 76.

[178]Ibid., p. 83.

[179]Ibid., p. 86.

Contrary to Strauss, Locke did not pervert natural law: he developed further a common medieval understanding, exactly as Rothbard maintained. True enough, Thomas Aquinas, the foremost thinker of the Middle Ages, made no use of subjective rights. But the great sixteenth-century Salamancan scholastic Francisco de Vitoria found it an easy task to devise a natural rights theory on a Thomistic basis. Once more, Strauss is confuted.

Strauss's rejection of individual rights led him to espouse political views that Rothbard found repellent.

> We find Strauss praising . . . "farsighted," "sober" British imperialism; we find him discoursing on the "good" Caesarism, on Caesarism as often necessary and not really tyranny, etc. . . . he praises political philosophers for, yes, lying to their readers for the sake of the "social good." . . . I must say that this is an odd position for a supposed moralist to take.[180]

Not only did Rothbard oppose Strauss's anti-individualist account of natural law; he also found risible the method of textual analysis by which Strauss arrived at his conclusions. Strauss believed that the great political philosophers faced a dilemma. They often held views at odds with prevailing orthodoxy; should they propagate their dissent openly, they faced persecution. In any case, their doctrines were meant for an elite group of disciples, not for an unlearned public unfit to judge them.

What then was to be done? According to Strauss, the philosophers concealed their true opinions through esoteric writing. Seeming contradictions in the text of a great philosopher were not mistakes; they instead signaled the presence of a hidden message.

Rothbard, to say the least, found Strauss's thesis unpersuasive. Strauss's most extended presentation of esoteric interpretation is

---

[180]Letter to Kenneth Templeton, January 23, 1960; Rothbard Papers; in Modugno, ed., *Diritto, natura e ragione*, p. 115.

contained in his *Thoughts on Machiavelli*.[181] About this work Rothbard comments:

> But it is one thing to look for circumspection, and quite
> another to construct a veritable architectonic of myth and
> conjecture based on the assumption of Machiavelli as an
> omniscient Devil, writing on a dozen different levels of "hid-
> den meaning." The Straussian ratiocination is generally so
> absurd as to be a kind of scholarly version of the Great Pyra-
> mid crackpots.[182]

Rothbard offered this as an example of Strauss's striving for esoteric novelty:

> Note the odd "reasoning": "Since the *Prince* consists of
> twenty-six chapters, and the *Prince* does not give us any infor-
> mation as to the possible meaning of this number, we turn to
> the twenty-sixth chapter of the *Discourses*." Note the "since,"
> as if this had the sweet logic of a syllogism.[183]

In defending his view of libertarian natural law, Rothbard confronted a challenge posed by Friedrich Hayek. Is not the attempt
to deduce from self-evident principles the precepts of law an example of the "constructivist rationalism" that has been a principal
enemy of liberty? Rothbard vigorously disagreed: Hayek in his
view was an irrationalist. In a review, written in 1958, of the manuscript of Hayek's *The Constitution of Liberty*,[184] Rothbard
expressed alarm. It is "surprisingly and distressingly, an extremely
bad, and I would even say evil, book."[185] For Rothbard, intellectual

---

[181]Leo Strauss, *Thoughts on Machiavelli* (Chicago: University of
Chicago Press, 1958).

[182]Letter to Ivan Bierly, February 9, 1960; Rothbard Papers; in
Modugno, ed., *Diritto, natura e ragione*, p. 118.

[183]Ibid., p. 119.

[184]Memorandum of January 21, 1958 on the unpublished manuscript
of Hayek, *The Constitution of Liberty*; Rothbard Papers; in Modugno, ed.,
Diritto, natura e ragione, pp. 77–78.

[185]Ibid., p. 77.

opponents often inhabited a dark landscape. He could apply to himself the words of Dante: *Per me si va ne la citta dolente* [Through me is the way to the sorrowful city].[186]

Hayek's account of natural law and reason lay at the heart of Rothbard's critique:

> Tied up with his dismissal of natural law is Hayek's continu-ous, and all-pervasive, attack on reason. Reason is his bête noire, and time and time again, from numerous and even contradictory standpoints, he opposes it. The true rationalist theory was, and is, that reason can discover the natural law of man, and from this can discover the natural rights of liberty. Since Hayek dismisses this even from historical considera-tion, he is left with only two choices for the formation of a political ethic: *either* blind adherence to custom and the tra-ditions of the "social organism," *or* the coercive force of gov-ernment edict.[187]

To Rothbard, Hayek's rejection of reason led to muddleheaded and unlibertarian views. Besides the very long list of such measures that Rothbard cites in a later review,[188] he also notes that Hayek was prepared to support conscription, if needed to defend against an external enemy.[189] In *The Constitution of Liberty*, Hayek surpris-ingly criticized the Supreme Court for finding too many of Roo-sevelt's New Deal measures unconstitutional.[190] This anomaly in a supposedly libertarian work did not escape Rothbard's attention.

---

[186]Dante, *Inferno*, Canto 3, line 1.

[187]Rothbard Papers, review of Hayek, *Constitution of Liberty*; empha-sis in the original; Modugno, ed, *Diritto, natura e ragione*, p. 80.

[188]Rothbard Papers; Modugno, ed, *Diritto, natura e ragione*, pp. 108–12.

[189]Rothbard Papers; Modugno, ed, *Diritto, natura e ragione*, p. 44.

[190]Hayek, *The Constitution of Liberty*, p. 190.

In another letter about Hayek, Rothbard challenges the dominant orthodoxy in contemporary political philosophy. Hayek agrees with critics of the free market that people do not deserve the incomes they receive. But this is not, in his view, a failure of the market. We have no objective means to assess the moral merits of people, so moral desert cannot properly be a principle of distribution.

Rothbard dissents:

> Hayek errs by denying that a free market apportions income in accordance with merit. His argument is that since we know nothing, we can't know what a person's merit is. . . . But all he needed to do was to realize that "merit" in this sense simply means merit in the production of goods and services exchangeable on the market. Income is then apportioned in proportion to this productivity. [191]

To this, Hayek would reply that people do not "really" deserve the value of what they produce, since arbitrary factors lie behind the abilities people possess to contribute to production. Rothbard "submit[s] that this is sheer nonsense." Hayek has conjured up a notion of "merit" that he has not defined and used this to challenge the justice of distribution by results. He then says that distribution cannot be in accord with "merit" in his sense: but this is true only because he has characterized the concept in such a vague way that one can never tell whether it has been satisfied. Rothbard, with his characteristic insistence on clarity, finds no use for Hayek's concept.

Rothbard has here gone beyond Robert Nozick. In responding to Rawls's claim that people do not deserve their earnings on the market, Nozick responded that they might still be entitled to these earnings. Rothbard asks: why stop with this? Why not say that people *do* deserve the market value of what they produce?

---

[191]Letter to Richard C. Cornuelle, October 23, 1956; Rothbard Papers.

He raises another decisive challenge to Hayek:

> He does not really come to grips with the problem of equality, and of such a concept violating the nature of man. Instead, he keeps talking about the advantages to "society" of permitting the inequalities. Always the emphasis is on "society" rather than the individual. . . . Here Hayek is committing the sin of holism which he has in the past so well condemned.[192]

In criticizing Hayek, Rothbard warned against resting the case for freedom exclusively on man's ignorance. Doing so is "flimsy enough for someone like Willmoore Kendall to drive a ten-ton truck through."[193] Rothbard respected this idiosyncratic conservative theorist; and his criticism of Kendall is one of the treasures of his unpublished papers.

Kendall assailed the Liberal Left for its elitism. Liberal intellectuals presumed themselves to be morally superior to the masses and entitled to rule them, while wishing to preserve the formal trappings of democracy. But, Kendall maintained, there were no "moral experts." Experts were of value only as technicians to tell us how to achieve a given set of goals. The settled conservative convictions of the American people should determine policy: the "deliberate sense of the community," not the arbitrary preferences of the Liberal Left, should guide us. Communists and other radicals have no rights to freedom of speech. All communities rest on an orthodoxy that may, if necessary, be enforced on dissenters.

Rothbard, after attending lectures by Kendall at Buck Hill Falls, reported that he was "a very keen and stimulating thinker, incisive, and with a sharply radical spirit, i.e., a propensity to dig to the roots of issues without fear or favor."[194] Although he asked the right questions, his answers were dangerous mistakes.

---

[192]Ibid.

[193]Ibid.

[194]Unpublished report, September 1956; Rothbard Papers.

Kendall is right to protest the tyranny of the expert, but he himself has uncritically accepted the supposed dichotomy between fact and value. Kendall assumes that one person's preferences is as valid as another's. There cannot, then, be experts about the ends of morality. But how does Kendall know this?

> His [Kendall's] . . . major solution seems to be to hammer home the distinction between fact and value, to convince everyone that experts are only experts on facts and scientific laws, while every citizen should choose policy on the basis of which means will lead to his ends.[195]

Rothbard rejects Kendall's contention.

> He assumes that morally, everyone is equal and therefore the democratic census can decide. Why? Why is there not a "moral roster," even though a separate one from an "intellectual roster" [of experts]?[196]

Kendall has uncritically embraced moral relativism and subjectivism.

Kendall claims that a society has the right to preserve the orthodoxy that governs it, but Rothbard finds his argument wanting. He considers Kendall's striking claim that the Athenian Assembly rightly condemned Socrates to death:

> If the Athenians were so damn committed to their way of life, they had little to worry about; and if Socrates were really becoming a threat, then they were no longer particularly committed to their way of life.[197]

Suppose Kendall were to acknowledge this point, but still wanted to suppress dissent. Then, contrary to his claim, he is not

---

[195]Ibid.

[196]Ibid.

[197]Ibid.

really a partisan of majority rule. Returning to Socrates and the Athenians, Rothbard comments:

> If they [the Athenian Assembly] are so worried—and Kendall intimates that they are so worried—because they are afraid that enough of their number will be converted until, say, 55 percent of the Athenians will become Socratics . . . then at least 45 percent of the Athenians must not be passionately committed, must be in danger of seceding to the enemy. But if that is the case, Kendall is *not* defending the right and duty of the majority to suppress a minority; he is defending the right and duty of a *minority* to suppress a possible majority.[198]

Kendall's position is more than an intellectual mistake. To put into practice the rule by popular opinion that he favors would destroy freedom and with it, civilization itself. If any group that believes itself to know the truth can suppress dissent, change becomes impossible:

> Since every new social change of importance is subversive of the old order, and disturbs people's minds for a while, Kendall must keep going back and back, since every society originated in a revolution against some preceding society. In short, Kendall's ethical philosophy must lead back to where—to the era of the cave man. . . . If Kendall has set forth the philosophy of tyranny cogently, we see that philosophy leads to: the end of civilization and most of the human race—in short, the death-principle.[199]

Rothbard's power as a critic is here on full display.

If Rothbard rejected this appeal to consensus and orthodoxy, he viewed the tyranny of the Liberal Left with no more favor than did Kendall. In a review of Charles L. Black, Jr., *The People and the Court: Judicial Review in a Democracy*,[200] he praised Black for exposing a key tactic of the elitists. Black, a major figure at the Yale Law

---

[198]Ibid.; emphasis in the original.

[199]Ibid.

[200]Charles L. Black, Jr., *The People and the Court: Judicial Review in a Democracy* (New York: Macmillan, 1960).

School, wrote as a committed advocate of elitism. In Black's view, the Supreme Court played a crucial role in validating the growth of government and the restriction of economic liberty. By convincing the public that government policy was "legitimate," the Court disarmed potential resistance to elite rule:

> Now, judicial review, beloved by conservatives, can of course fulfill the excellent function of declaring government interventions and tyrannies unconstitutional. But it can *also* validate and legitimize the government in the eyes of the people by declaring these actions valid and *constitutional*. Thus, the courts and the Supreme Court become an instrument of spearheading and confirming Federal tyranny instead of the reverse. . . . Professor Black's contribution here is to see and understand this process.[201]

According to Black, it is especially important for Americans to be convinced that the government is legitimate:

> The United States was set up as a limited government, and given the originally sovereign states, it could *only* have begun as a strictly limited government. . . . It is therefore particularly important, writes Black shrewdly, for a limited government to convince and cajole people that it is acting with legitimacy—so that even the most hostile critics of its actions will, down deep, accept the government itself. Herein lies the particular function of the Supreme Court.[202]

An obvious objection can be raised to Black's analysis. True enough, the Court can act to validate government power; its occasional declarations that the government has acted unconstitutionally can be seen, just as Black alleges, as "window dressing" to secure popular compliance. But does this not depend on the personnel of the Court? Can one not imagine a conservative Court that would act to protect liberty?

---

[201]Letter to Kenneth Templeton, March 24, 1961; Rothbard Papers; emphasis in the original.

[202]Ibid.

The suggestion is chimerical; structural reasons militate against it. As Black rightly notes,

> it is illogical to have the State itself—through its Supreme Court—be recognized as the final and sole judge of its own (State) actions. . . . [John C.] Calhoun saw the problem with beautiful clarity.[203]

Black refuses to abandon judicial review, even though he acknowledges that "he puts his faith in 'something of a miracle' of government being judge of its own cause," because he cannot accept the obvious alternative.

> But, says, Black, what is the alternative? The Calhoun alternative . . . was nullification, interposition, movements toward unanimity principles, etc., but Black instantly . . . rejects this sort of route as leading to an anarchic negation of the national government itself.[204]

To Rothbard, the horrible outcome that Black fears is precisely what we need. He concludes with an important statement of his view of the Constitution:

> the Constitution, regarded as an attempt to limit government, was one of the most noble attempts . . . at curbing the State in human history—but . . . it has failed, and failed almost ignominiously. One reason for such failure, as Calhoun predicted, is the monopoly Supreme Court.[205]

In his unpublished reports, Rothbard of course did not neglect his principal academic specialty. He acutely criticized mainstream work in economics and economic history. Although James Buchanan approached advocacy of the free market more closely than most economists, Rothbard could not accept his methodology. It was based on unrealistic assumptions; and Rothbard deftly exposes a central weakness.

---

[203]Ibid.

[204]Ibid.

[205]Ibid.

In a review of a book by Buchanan and two coauthors, *Prices, Incomes, and Public Policy*,[206] Rothbard states that "this book brings home to me as few have done how much can go wrong if one's philosophical approach—one's epistemology—is all wrong."[207]

What is this central error?

> At the root of almost all the troubles of the book lies the weak, confused, and inconsistent *positivism*: the willingness to use false assumptions if their "predictive value" seems to be of some use. It is this crippling positivist willingness to let anything slip by, to *not* be rigorous about one's theory because "the assumptions don't have to be true or realistic anyway" that permeates and ruins this book.[208]

Here Rothbard, as usual, settles upon a vital point. One might be inclined to object to Rothbard by saying, what, after all, is wrong with using false assumptions? Are they not useful as first approximations? If we can arrive at a theory that predicts well, its assumptions can be refined to make them more realistic.

Ernest Nagel took exactly this position:

> If you're going to develop an adequate theory . . . you must simplify, idealize, and even make assumptions *that are clearly contrary to known existing fact!!* This is necessary to develop a body of theory. . . simply for the sake of analytic convenience. The empirical justification of this is the ability to introduce supplementary assumptions later that will bring it close to the facts.[209]

---

[206]James M. Buchanan, Clark Lee Allen, and Marshall R. Colberg, *Prices, Incomes, and Public Policy: The ABC's of Economics* (New York: McGraw-Hill, 1954).

[207]Letter to Ivan Bierly, February 3, 1960; Rothbard Papers.

[208]Ibid.

[209]Notes on Nagel lectures, September 1948; Rothbard Papers; emphasis in the original.

Rothbard disagreed with his teacher, and his counterargument strikes to the heart of the matter. He maintains that the use of false assumptions in economics has in practice weakened theoretical rigor. Whatever the rationale of Nagel and other positivists, the use of false assumptions has had malign effects: "For if a theory or analysis doesn't have to be strictly true or coherently united to other theory, then almost anything goes—all to be justified with 'predictive value' or some other such excuse."[210]

He documents his point to the hilt in his consideration of Buchanan's book, and the criticisms he offers apply far beyond their immediate target. Buchanan and his coauthors talk about monopoly, even though they

> sense there is something wrong with the whole current theory of monopoly, that it is even impossible to *define* monopoly cogently, or define monopoly of a commodity. But while they see these things, they never do anything about it, or start from there to construct an economics that will stand up— because they are thoroughly misled by their positivist attitude of "well, this might be a useful tool for some purposes."[211]

In like fashion, these authors use the "fashionable jargon" of short-run cost curves of the firm. They recognize that

> it is all rather arbitrary; this they brush aside with the retort that it can have some "predictive value." The term that I think best describes the shoddiness and eclecticism induced by this philosophic approach is "irresponsibility."[212]

Bad theory leads to bad policy. Just as Rothbard deplored sloppy theoretical assumptions, so did he protest against vague and unsupported ethical premises. "The same grave philosophical confusion permits them to suddenly slip their own ethical assumptions into the book, undefended, and practically unannounced." On

---

[210]Ibid.

[211]Letter to Ivan Bierly, February 3, 1960; Rothbard Papers.

[212]Ibid.

what basis do they assume that perfect competition and equality are "good things"?

Rothbard notes an anomalous feature of the egalitarian policy favored by these authors and common elsewhere:

> And they have even the further colossal gall to denounce "price discrimination" (e.g., doctors charging more to the rich than to the poor) because it is, for some reason, terribly unethical for private people to engage in their own strictly voluntary redistribution of wealth . . . it is *only* legitimate for the government to effect this redistribution by coercion. This ethical nonsense they don't feel they have to defend. . . . It is this kind of slipshod, unphilosophic sophomoric "ethics" that is again typical of the Chicago School in action.[213]

Rothbard obviously found maddening this casual attitude to conceptual rigor; and on one occasion he directly confronted Buchanan over it. He was "appalled" by the use of a "fixed-demand" curve. He devised a counterexample to show the absurdity of the concept.

> The authors said that a fixed, vertical demand curve is illustrated by the government's demand for soldiers, and that if not enough people volunteer, the government will draft the rest . . . the analysis is nonsense, since if say the government wants 100,000 men in the army but if so many people are 4-F or exempt that only 60,000 can possibly be hired or drafted, we then have a vertical supply and vertical demand curve which can never intersect. On the authors' own premises, then, *no one* would be in the army, which is clearly absurd.[214]

Much to Rothbard's dismay, Buchanan conceded his point. In a letter that Rothbard quotes, he replied: "You [Rothbard] are quite right in saying that the solution . . . under your assumptions is

---

[213]Ibid.; emphasis in the original.
[214]Ibid.; emphasis in the original.

absurd. But this is really the same in all of those cases in which we make rather extreme assumptions."[215] Rothbard threw up his hands in horror:

> now, it seems to me that this kind of philosophy, this posi-
> tivistic approach to economic theory, corrupts it, if I may use
> so strong a term, at the very core, and that no theory of last-
> ing merit can emerge from this sort of cauldron.[216]

Unfortunately, Rothbard's insistence on absolute conceptual rigor has thus far remained a minority view.

Buchanan was of course a pioneer in "public choice" econom-ics; and both he and Gordon Tullock greatly admired Anthony Downs's classic in this area, *An Economic Theory of Democracy*.[217] Rothbard did not. He found in Downs's work the same mistaken use of false assumptions that he condemned in Buchanan.

> Its key fallacy is in adopting the fashionable positivism of our
> day, which asserts that a theory resting on *false* assumptions can
> be good and worthwhile, if it can make good "predictions"
> based on "testable" propositions. This ignores the fact that in
> human action, propositions are not "testable" in this way.[218]

As usual, Rothbard is not satisfied with a general condemna-tion. He shows in detail how Downs's error in theory derails his book. Downs makes arbitrary assumptions about rational action; he "proceeds throughout the book judging some actions as 'rational', others as 'irrational' etc., all mind you, under the guise of not making ethical value judgments."[219]

---

[215]Ibid.

[216]Ibid.

[217]Anthony Downs, *An Economic Theory of Democracy* (New York: Harper, 1957).

[218]Letter to Ivan Bierly, August 26, 1959; Rothbard Papers; empahsis in the original.

[219]Ibid.

Rothbard has little use for Downs's various predictive hypotheses, finding them vague or erroneous. One example must here suffice:

> the flat statement is made, without qualification: "A vote against any party is not a vote against government *per se* but net disapproval of the marginal actions that party has taken."
> . . . When I [Rothbard] vote, I vote against government *per se* sometimes; this action is enough to refute Downs.[220]

Downs has condemned anarchists to analytical oblivion through an arbitrary assumption.

Rothbard quickly dispatched another future winner of the Nobel Prize in a review of Robert Fogel's *The Union Pacific Railroad*.[221] Fogel argued that the Crédit Mobilier promoters were not swindlers.

> From the point of view of "social return," the railroad was eminently profitable and worthwhile. Fogel celebrates the railroads and its effects; and the famous swindling of the Crédit Mobilier promoters is dismissed as a myth, as profits no more than justified by the "risk" to the promoters.[222]

To Rothbard, Fogel's entire line of argument rested on a fundamental fallacy.

> I am not impressed, however, with a point of view that worries about the "entrepreneurial risk" assumed by people who receive the largesse of government bonds, and who wonder at what price they can resell the bonds on the market.[223]

---

[220]Ibid.

[221]Robert Fogel, *The Union Pacific Railroad: A Case of Premature Enterprise* (Baltimore: Johns Hopkins, 1960).

[222]Letter to Kenneth Templeton, June 26, 1961.

[223]Ibid.

Fogel failed to distinguish between genuine investment on the market and "investment" subsidized by the government. To equate the two showed a lack a conceptual clarity.

Fogel's mistake reflected a preference for government control of the economy:

> Fogel concludes that the Union Pacific construction was a fine, noble work for the general welfare; he would have preferred, however that the railroad were built *totally* as a government enterprise, so the costs would have been at a minimum, and government could have reaped the profit for "entrepreneurial risk," at which point government could have sold the railroad, at a capitalized value, to private enterprise.[224]

Rothbard, with characteristic depth, here reverts to a familiar theme. Just as in welfare economics, lack of conceptual clarity—in the case the equation of private with government risk—leads to antimarket views.

Rothbard saw Fogel's pattern of reasoning as part of a larger trend among American historians.

> This book, in its whitewashing of the Crédit Mobilier scandals, is indicative of a perhaps broader movement in American historiography: with the shift of left-wing American historians from Marxism or straight socialism to belief in a "mixed economy," the value placed by these historians in "muckraking" has dwindled very sharply.[225]

Corruption almost always involves cooperation between government and business interests; thus, those who support a mixed economy, which favors such cooperation, will tend to ignore corruption. "Muckraking, on the other hand, is suitable *either* for 100% socialist historians *or* for libertarians." Rothbard not only explains Fogel's lapse but identifies a key area of his own historical practice:

---

[224]Ibid.; emphasis in the original.
[225]Ibid.

few things interested him more than the malign partnership of government and business.

Another future Nobel laureate received much more detailed scrutiny. In his analysis of Douglass North's *The Economic Growth of the United States, 1790–1860*,[226] we see Rothbard at the height of his critical powers. Rothbard's demolition may at first seem surprising, as North is taken in most quarters to be a strong supporter of the free market. But to Rothbard, conceptual clarity and rigor are, as ever, foremost; the mistakes of supposed friends of the market could be more deadly than the efforts of professed enemies. Rothbard, like the protagonist of Ibsen's *Brand*, could say, "The Devil is compromise!"

Rothbard once more finds that errors in method lead to errors in policy. North lacks an adequate view of causation: he does not grasp that individuals act. Instead, he thinks mechanically, asking for the mathematical relationships between certain variables.

> North, like all scientistic-minded historians, has, at bottom, a highly mechanical and deterministic view of economic growth. There are resources, there are export industries . . . and there are various "multiplier-accelerator" models of impact of these various export industries. The role of individuals acting, of entrepreneurs and innovators, North deliberately and frankly deprecates; the role of capital investment—so crucial [to] development—receives similar slighting treatment.[227]

Thus, North notes, accurately enough, that in developing countries, exports industries play a crucial role. But, owing to his mechanistic views, he reverses the direction of causation:

> North has seen the obvious fact that, generally, the most advanced industry, especially in an "underdeveloped" country, is a leading *export* industry. But he concludes from this

---

[226]Douglass North, *The Economic Growth of the United States, 1790–1860* (New York: W.W. Norton, 1966).

[227]Letter to Ivan Bierly, May 1, 1961; Rothbard Papers.

that there is something powerful and uniquely spurring to development of an export industry *per se*. In short, instead of realizing that an industry which is particularly efficient and advanced *will then become* a leading export industry, he tends to reverse the proper causation and attribute almost mystic powers of initiating development, etc., to export industries *per se*.[228]

Rothbard relentlessly shows how this initial error leads to further mistakes. North thinks that export industries are a "good thing," without asking how they arise: he goes on to suggest that an export industry that spends its profits on imports is less beneficial to development than one that spends its receipts at home. His reasoning has a certain logic to it: if exports, as such, are good, should they not remain undiluted by imports?

But the premise, once more, is false: exports are not an absolute good. North has revived a mercantilist fallacy:

> He claims . . . that an export industry the receipts of which are then used largely for imports leak away, and hinder development of the country; whereas, export industries where the spending "stays at home," builds up the country, because it retains within the country the "multiplier-accelerator" effects of such spending. This Keynesian nonsense applied even beyond where Keynes would apply it—i.e., to all situations and not just depressions.[229]

Rothbard now applies one of his favorite critical techniques, which we have several times seen in operation. He pushes an author's reasoning to an extreme, in order to show its absurdity. Thus, North claims that if a region has only one export industry, development will be impeded. But he offers no definition of "region"—as ever, Rothbard demands precision. What is the upshot?

---

[228]Ibid.; emphasis in the original.
[229]Ibid.

North (who realizes that regions are as important an economic unit as the politically artificial "nation") talks of
"regions" tied to one export. And yet how big or small is a
"region"? "Region" is an economically meaningless term, as
we can make the "region" small enough so that it could
never have more than one export commodity. And yet this
does not make such a region poor or underdeveloped.[230]

Errors in theory have grave consequences:

The logic of North's position, which apparently he does not
carry through, is basically protectionist; industry is weighted
more highly than other goods, exports more highly than
other industries, etc. . . . So protection minded is North that
he actually says that an export commodity which requires
more investment in capital facilities, etc. is better and more
conducive to growth than one requiring less, because there
will be more spending on home port facilities, etc. This again
is protectionistic nonsense.[231]

Rothbard is careful to add that North himself does not draw the
policy implications of his own analysis; he does not state a position
about protective tariffs. What interests Rothbard, though, is the
logic of the argument: here, he says, is where one will be pushed to
go, if one falls into this fallacy.

But why is it a fallacy? Rothbard identifies the basic Keynesian
error:

it [North's argument's on capital investment] claims that a
less efficient, and less productive industry is better than a
more efficient and more productive because more money is
spent by the former on costs, resources, etc. Isn't the money
that is saved ever used?[232]

Beneath this Keynesian fallacy lies a deeper failing. Keynesian
reasoning is just one example of an attempt to "force" the market.

---

[230]Ibid.
[231]Ibid.
[232]Ibid.

Industrial development becomes an unexamined end-in-itself; but why is growth in this sector always desirable?

> Once again, the important desideratum is freedom of the market; a country or region will often best develop, depending on conditions of resources or the market, by concentrating on one or two items, and then exchanging them for other items produced elsewhere. If this comes in a free market, it is far more productive than forcing a hothouse steel or textile mill in the name of "economic growth."[233]

North in this instance does not himself take the fatal step into false policy—most economists do manage to avoid recommending tariffs, regardless of what their argument requires. In another area, though, North allows an unexamined ethical assumption to skew his analysis. He notes, accurately enough, that some plantation economies are underdeveloped, and that such economies are also highly inegalitarian. Probably because of his own commitment to equality, he wrongly concludes inequality is bad for development:

> Unequal distribution of income he associates with a "plantation" economy, where the planners have the ill grace to spend their money on imported luxuries; this is contrasted to the noble, more egalitarian economy where more people develop home industry and home activities. Once again, North's position is compounded of both historical and economic errors; the fact that, historically, some plantation systems had unequal incomes *does* not mean that either the plantation system or the inequality [always] inhibited economic development. Certainly neither did.[234]

Rothbard's reports on economic works were by no means always negative. He declared that Lawrence Abbott's *Quality and Competition*[235] was a masterpiece. Most mainstream economists, in

---

[233]Ibid.

[234]Ibid.; emphasis in the original.

[235]Lawrence Abbott, *Quality and Competition* (New York: Columbia University Press, 1955).

pursuit of the chimera of perfect competition, deprecate product differentiation and advertising. Why, e.g., should there be different kinds of toothpaste or different brands of aspirin? Are not brands simply an attempt to restrict competition in selling the "same" commodity?

To this, defenders of the market, not least Rothbard himself, were before Abbott's book inclined to answer just by insisting on the fact that people had freely chosen to accept the products offered to them. But no one had been able to give a theoretically satisfying account of "quality" competition.

> Before this [book] economists, including myself have thought that *theory* need not account specially for quality because a different quality good for the same price is equivalent to a different price for the same good. A different quality, would, further, be simply treated as a different good for most purposes, the same for others. Up till now, no one has been able to distinguish, theoretically, between a different quality and a different good.[236]

Abbott solved this theoretical conundrum by asking, which want does a good satisfy? Products that satisfy the same want count as goods of the same kind. Differences in such products are differences in quality of the same good, not different goods altogether.

> Abbott furnishes an excellent distinction based upon the thesis that the same good satisfies the same *want*, so that there can be quality variations within the same want . . . using this stress on class of wants, he can show (in the Austrian tradition) that a greater variety of goods or an increasing standard of living, fulfills more wants, or fulfills them with greater precision and accuracy than before.[237]

---

[236]Letter to Kenneth Templeton, July 21, 1958; Rothbard Papers; emphasis in the original.

[237]Ibid.; emphasis in the original.

Given this innovation, it hardly comes as a surprise that Abbott defends quality competition.

> Abbott shows that quality competition is *not* only not a poor substitute for price competition, as modern theorists proclaim, but essential to what he calls "complete competition, which combines price and quality competition" . . . he stresses the value for competition of brand names, advertising (to satisfy consumer wants more fully and give them more information), [and] diversity of product.[238]

Despite Rothbard's advocacy, the book never attracted much attention. But Rothbard continued to admire it, and he several times cites it in *Man, Economy, and State*.[239]

ROTHBARD'S SYSTEM OF ETHICS

Although Rothbard usually found himself in close agreement with Mises, in one area he maintained that Mises was mistaken. Mises contended that ethical judgments were subjective: ultimate ends are not subject to rational assessment. Rothbard dissented, maintaining that an objective ethics could be founded on the requirements of human nature. His approach, based on his study of Aristotelian and Thomist philosophy, is presented in his major work *The Ethics of Liberty*,[240] his most important study of political philosophy.

Even if Rothbard is right that an objective ethics is possible, is this view essential to libertarianism? Why abandon Mises?

---

[238]Ibid.; emphasis in the original.

[239]*Man, Economy, and State with Power and Market*, pp. 666, 701, 730, 979.

[240]*The Ethics of Liberty* (1982; New York: New York University Press, 1998).

According to Mises, we can defend the free market without resorting to any controversial assumptions about the nature of ethics. One can demonstrate, without making any value judgments, that interventionist measures such as minimum wage laws fail to achieve the goals of their own advocates. If so, we have a value free defense of resistance to such measures and the free market is vindicated. Does this not suffice?

Rothbard did not think so. As he points out, interventionist measures do help some people, albeit at the expense of others. Labor unions, e.g., may raise the wages of their members, while causing others outside the union to lose their jobs. Why should one think that this result is, from the point of view of the union members, unsatisfactory? Contrary to Mises, then, interventionist measures do not always fail to attain the goals of their advocates. A value-free defense of the market cannot then stand by itself.

Rothbard first indicated his differences from Mises in a comment on Mises's paper, "Epistemological Relativism in the Sciences of Human Action," delivered at a Symposium on Relativism sponsored by the Volker Fund. He states his essential criticism forcefully:

> But how can Mises know what motivates the statists? Suppose, for example, the price controller wants power, and doesn't care if it creates shortages . . . (or is a nihilist and hates everyone, and wants to create shortages); suppose that someone who wants to confiscate the rich has a very high time preference and doesn't *care* if the economy will be wrecked in twenty years. What then?[241]

In Rothbard's ethical system, self-ownership is the basic principle; each person rightfully owns his or her own body. Few libertarians would dissent; but few, if any, have seen the implications of this principle so clearly as Rothbard.

---

[241]Rothbard's comment on Mises's paper at Volker Fund Symposium; Rothbard Papers; emphasis in the original.

To many libertarians, freedom of contract is the be-all and end-all. Rothbard disagrees: unlimited freedom of contract, far from being a consequence of self-ownership, in fact contradicts it. Given self-ownership, and acquisition of property through "mixing one's labor" with unowned property, one of course may freely enter into all sorts of agreements with others. Nevertheless, unlimited "freedom of contract" is unacceptable.

> Unfortunately, many libertarians, devoted to the right to make contracts, hold the *contract itself* to be an absolute, and therefore maintain that *any* voluntary contract whatever must be legally enforceable in the free society. Their error is a failure to realize that the right to contract is strictly derivable from the right of private property, and that therefore the only *enforceable* contracts . . . should be those where the failure of one party to abide by the contract implies the theft of property from the other party.[242]

It follows from Rothbard's understanding of contract that one cannot sell oneself into slavery. One can voluntarily submit to the will of another; but no legal force can compel someone to remain faithful to such a submission; to reiterate, contract does not stand as an absolute. Here, as is often the case, Rothbard disagrees with Robert Nozick, who held that contracts to sell oneself into slavery could be enforced.

Rothbard uses the principle of self-ownership to solve a complicated problem of legal theory. What is the basis for enforcing a contract? According to some legal theorists, including such eminent figures as Oliver Wendell Holmes and Roscoe Pound, a contract is in essence a promise. A variant of this position holds that a contract leads the parties to expect behavior of a specified kind. They accordingly plan their own actions and suffer loss if their expectations are disappointed. To help ensure that expectations are met, contracts may be enforced.

---

[242] *The Ethics of Liberty*, p. 133; emphasis in the original.

Rothbard easily dispatches these theories. Both contract-as-promise and contract-as-fulfilled expectation negate self-ownership: one may alienate only one's property, not one's will. He draws the drastic, but strictly logical, consequence that no promise as such can be enforced. Every legally binding contract must involve a transfer of titles between the parties at the time the contract is made.

His conclusion follows from his premise; but why accept the axiom of self-ownership, as Rothbard interprets it? He argues that all societies confront three alternatives: each person owns himself, some persons own others, or each person owns a part of everyone else. (Are these alternatives mutually exhaustive? Variants and combinations of the second and third may readily be devised, but these require no change in the fundamentals of Rothbard's argument.)

George Mavrodes objected that Rothbard had made an unwarranted assumption. Rothbard asks, who should own people? But why assume that people should be owned at all? As Rothbard uses the concept of ownership, however, Mavrodes's question lacks a point. By "ownership," Rothbard means "control"; and it is indeed the case that someone (or group) must control each person. Rothbard's alternatives cannot be escaped.

Given these alternatives, which should one choose? In his response, Rothbard relies heavily on a point of fact. Everyone is in reality in control of his own will. If I obey another, I must always make the decision to do as he wishes; and the threat of violence on his part should I follow my own course leaves the situation unchanged. I must decide whether to accede to the threat.

But, one might object, even if Rothbard is correct that one cannot alienate the will, how does he get to the conclusion he wants? From the fact that the will cannot be alienated, how does the ethical judgment follow that each person ought to be recognized as a self-owner? Is Rothbard here committing the fallacy of deriving an "ought" from an "is"?

To our imagined objector, Rothbard would demur. He does indeed derive an "ought" from an "is," but he would deny that he is guilty of any fallacy. He maintains that ethical principles follow from the nature of man. The fact that each person has control of his own will implies that the attempt to coerce the will of another is unjustifiable—to do so is to attempt to violate human nature. This prohibition does not apply, Rothbard holds, once violence has been initiated. Here one may respond with all necessary force, and Rothbard carefully elaborates a theory of retributive punishment.

Once self-ownership has been established, property rights soon follow: one acquires property through "mixing one's labor" with unowned property, or by acquiring such property in gift or exchange from someone else. Rothbard displays great dialectical skill in anticipating objections to his theory. One of the most important of these is that if one may acquire property through Lockean labor mixture, does this not unfairly bias matters in favor of the first possessor? Imagine a group of shipwrecked sailors swimming toward an uninhabited island. Does the first person to reach the island acquire it? Can he then refuse entry to his shipmates, unless they pay exorbitant rents to him? The political philosopher G.A. Cohen later raised exactly this objection to libertarianism, without reference to Rothbard's discussion.[243]

Rothbard easily turns aside the objection.

> Crusoe, landing upon a large island, may grandiosely trumpet to the winds his "ownership" of the entire island. But, in natural fact, he *owns* only the part that he settles and transforms into use. . . . Note that we are *not* saying that, in order for property in land to be valid, it must be *continually* in use. The only requirement is that the land be *once* put in use, and thus become the property of the one who has mixed his labor with, who imprinted the stamp of his personal energy upon, the land.[244]

---

[243]See G.A. Cohen, *Self-Ownership, Freedom, and Equality* (Cambridge: Cambridge University Press, 1995).

[244]*Ethics of Liberty*, p. 64; emphasis in the original.

We may imagine another objection at this point. Suppose Rothbard has successfully rebutted the contention of Georgists and others that first possessors of land can in his system hold to ransom all others. Is not the system, however logical, of no practical relevance? Most property titles today do not stem by a clear line of transmission from a Lockean first owner. On the contrary, would we not find that many land titles go back to acts of violent dispossession? Would not an attempt to put Rothbard's system in practice quickly lead to a war of conflicting claims to property?

As usual, Rothbard has thought of the objection himself. He answers that the burden of proof lies on someone who disputes a land title to make good his claim. If he cannot do so, the present possessor owns his land legitimately. If land titles cannot be traced back to an original act of legitimate appropriation, speculation about an original owner and his present descendants is idle.

But what if the objector *can* make good his claim? Then Rothbard is entirely prepared to follow out the implications of his system. Many landowners in Latin America and elsewhere would in a Rothbardian world find themselves in very much reduced circumstances:

> [A] *truly* free market, a truly libertarian society devoted to justice and property rights, can only be established there [in the underdeveloped world] by ending unjust feudal claims to property. But utilitarian economists, grounded on no ethical theory of property rights, can only fall back on defending whatever status quo may happen to exist.[245]

Rothbard's *Ethics* is in one sense mistitled. He sharply distinguishes political philosophy from ethics as a whole, and his book is addressed principally to the former topic.[246]

---

[245] Ibid., p. 70; emphasis in the original.

[246] Vittorio Hösle notes that this division is prominent in the political philosophy of Fichte. He held that cruelty to animals, e.g., though morally wrong, could not be banned by the state. *See* Vittorio Hösle, *Morals and Politics* (North Bend, Ind.: University of Notre Dame Press, 2004), p. 642.

When, e.g., he deduces from the nonaggression axiom that people ought to be free to make any voluntary exchange they wish, his conclusion, like his premise, is part of political philosophy. He makes no attempt to argue that every voluntary exchange is morally desirable. It follows, Rothbard contends, from sound political principles that blackmail ought not to be legally prohibited: it is the sale of the service of withholding information from interested parties. As another example of the iron consistency with which Rothbard is willing to pursue his conclusions in the face of commonly held beliefs, parents should be under no obligation to care for their infant children.

Some would at this point throw up their hands in outraged horror. But one may hope that before doing so, anyone who reacts negatively will consider the main issue. Rothbard in no way suggests that blackmail or parental neglect is morally permissible. His moral opinion of these practices is just the same as that of most people. But from the fact that an activity is immoral, it does not follow that it ought to be legally banned. Indeed if Rothbard is right about political morality, it will often be immoral to attempt to prohibit immoral activity. This seeming paradox, instead of undermining morality, actually serves as an important means for its defense. One has only to glance at any period of history to see that the main violator of morality has been what Nietzsche called "that coldest of all cold monsters, the State." A doctrine, like Rothbard's, that rigidly restricts the role of politics in the enforcement of morality can only be welcomed from the moral point of view.

A substantial part of *The Ethics of Liberty* is devoted to Rothbard's criticisms of other classical liberals, including Mises, Hayek, and Isaiah Berlin. His discussion of Robert Nozick is especially noteworthy. As he points out, a key part of Nozick's defense of a minimal state depends on an equivocation. Nozick's argument is a response to Rothbard's contention that, ideally, protective services should be provided by competing private agencies. A compulsory monopoly agency, i.e., a government, is neither necessary nor desirable.

Against Rothbard, Nozick deploys an argument that at first sight seems devastating. Grant Rothbard his private market anarchism, Nozick suggests. Then, in a way entirely consistent with Rothbard's system, a monopoly agency will spring up. Rothbard's system defeats itself.

Rising to the challenge, Rothbard locates a crucial weakness in Nozick's argument. Nozick concerns himself greatly with cases in which protection agencies clash over the appropriate procedure to use in trials of criminals. One outcome that Nozick canvasses is an agreement among the agencies to establish an appeals court.

So far Nozick is on the right lines, and Rothbard himself lays great stress on the need for agreements of exactly this kind. But, according to Nozick, agencies that thus come to agreement have coalesced into a single agency. Rothbard finds this step in Nozick's argument unreasonable: do disputing companies that agree to arbitration constitute by that agreement a single firm? Nozick has "refuted" Rothbard through the use of an arbitrary definition.

POLITICS IN THEORY AND PRACTICE

Rothbard modified the famous dictum of Marx: he wished both to understand and change the world. He endeavored to apply the ideas he had developed in his theoretical work to current politics and to bring libertarian views to the attention of the general public. One issue for him stood foremost. Like Randolph Bourne, he maintained that "war is the health of the state"; he accordingly opposed an aggressive foreign policy.

His support for nonintervention in foreign policy led him to champion the Old Right. John T. Flynn, Garet Garrett and other pre-World War II "isolationists" shared Rothbard's belief in the close connection between state power and bellicose foreign policy.

The situation was quite otherwise with postwar American conservatism. Although Rothbard was an early contributor to William

Buckley's *National Review*, he rejected the aggressive pursuit of the Cold War advocated by Buckley and such members of his editorial staff as James Burnham and Frank S. Meyer. He broke with these self-styled conservatives and thereafter became one of their strongest opponents. For similar reasons, he condemned their neoconservative successors.

Rothbard made clear the basis of his opposition to *National Review* foreign policy in an essay, "For a New Isolationism," written in April 1959; the magazine did not publish it. To those who favored a policy of "liberation" directed against the Communist bloc, Rothbard raised a devastating objection:

> In all the reams of material written by the Right in the last decade [1949–1959], there is never any precise spelling-out of what a policy of ultrafirmness or toughness really entails. Let us then fill in this gap by considering what I am sure is the *toughest possible* policy: an immediate ultimatum to Khrushchev and Co. to resign and disband the whole Communist regime; otherwise we drop the H-bomb on the Kremlin. . . . What is wrong with this policy? Simply that it would quickly precipitate an H-bomb, bacteriological, chemical, global war which would destroy the United States as well as Russia.[247]

To this dire picture, proponents of "rollback" would of course respond that the Communists would surrender: Rothbard dissents, for reasons that will be discussed in detail later. Suffice it to say here that he thought it obvious that since "the destruction of the United States would follow such an ultimatum, we must strongly oppose such a policy."[248]

If "liberation" leads to national suicide, what is the alternative? Rothbard suggests a return to "the ancient and traditional American policy of isolationism and neutrality." But is this not open to a

---

[247]Unpublished manuscript, "For a New Isolationism," April 1959; emphasis in the original.

[248]Ibid.

fatal objection? "But, I [Rothbard] will hear from every side, every-one knows that isolationism is obsolete and dead, in this age of H-bombs, guided missiles, etc."[249] How can America shun involve-ment in European power politics if Russia has the ability to destroy us? No longer can we retreat to Fortress America.

To this Rothbard has a simple response: "*a program of world dis-armament up to the point where isolationism again becomes militarily practical.*"[250] If this policy were carried out, America would be safe from foreign attack: no longer would we need to involve ourselves in foreign quarrels. Mutual disarmament was in Russia's interest as well, so a disarmament agreement was entirely feasible.

Ever alert for objections, Rothbard anticipates that critics will charge that a Fortress America would have crushing military expenses and be cut off from world trade. Not at all, he responds:

> this argument, never very sensible, is absurd today when we are groaning under the fantastic budgets imposed by our nuclear arms race. Certainly . . . our arms budget will be less than it is now. . . . The basis of all trade is benefit to *both* par-ties.[251]

Even if a hostile power controlled the rest of the world, why would it not be willing to trade with us? Unfortunately, Rothbard's argu-ments did not have any effect on his bellicose antagonists.

He followed a pragmatic policy of temporary alliances with whatever groups were, at a given time, opposed to militarism and foreign adventures. He set forward the basis for his political stance in a key essay, "Left and Right: The Prospects for Liberty."[252] This

---

[249]Ibid.

[250]Ibid.; emphasis in the original.

[251]Ibid.; emphasis in the original.

[252]"Left and Right: The Prospects for Liberty," *Left and Right* 1, no. 1 (Spring, 1965). Reprinted in *Egalitarianism as a Revolt Against Nature and Other Essays*, 2nd ed. (1974; Auburn, Ala.: Ludwig von Mises Institute, 2000).

appeared in an important scholarly journal, *Left and Right*, which he established. This contained major essays on revisionist history and foreign policy, but unfortunately lasted only from 1965–1968.

The key essay just mentioned is available in the collection *Egalitarianism as a Revolt Against Nature and Other Essays*, which contains some of Rothbard's most important work on political theory.

In the book's initial essay, whose title has been adopted for the whole book, he raises a basic challenge to the schools of economics and politics that dominate current opinion.[253] Almost everyone assumes that equality is a "good thing"; even proponents of the free market like Milton Friedman join this consensus. The dispute between conservatives and radicals centers on the terms of trade between equality and efficiency.

Rothbard utterly rejects the assumption on which this argument turns. Why assume that equality is desirable? It is not enough, he contends, to advocate it as a mere aesthetic preference, in the style of Frank Knight. Quite the contrary, egalitarians, like everyone else, need rationally to justify their ethical mandates.

To Rothbard, as we have seen in the discussion of *The Ethics of Liberty*, ethical justification requires attention to the requirements of human nature. Judged by this standard, the results are devastating for the egalitarian view. Everywhere in nature we find inequality. Attempts to remake human beings so that everyone fits into the same mold lead inevitably to tyranny.

> The great fact of individual difference and variability (that is, inequality) is evident from the long record of human experience; hence, the general recognition of the antihuman nature of a world of coerced uniformity.[254]

---

[253]The essay first appeared in *Modern Age* in 1973; Robert Nozick made exactly the same point in his article "Distributive Justice," which appeared in the same year, and in *Anarchy, State, and Utopia*, which appeared in the year following.

[254]*Egalitarianism as a Revolt Against Nature*, p. 8. The pursuit of *absolute* equality, it will be recalled, Rothbard has shown in *Power and Market* to be conceptually impossible.

Rothbard broadens and extends his criticism of equality in "Freedom, Inequality, Primitivism, and the Division of Labor."[255] Not only do biology and history make human beings inherently different from one another, but the division of labor springs from the fact that human beings vary in their abilities.

As we shall later see in the discussion of *An Austrian Perspective on the History of Economic Thought*,[256] Rothbard was an exceptionally keen critic of Marxism. Beginning with Marx's juvenile *Manuscripts of 1844*,[257] Marx and his successors have prated endlessly about the supposed horrors of the division of labor. In a capitalist economy, workers normally have only one specialty: plumbers, for example, are usually not doctors as well. Does not this specialization ensure that people in a capitalist economy are narrow and stunted? But socialism will change all that. In the millennium to come, everyone will be able freely to pursue a wide variety of careers: "the free development of each will be the condition for the free development of all."[258]

In response, Rothbard does not hesitate to call nonsense by its name. The very phenomenon that Marx deplores, the division of labor, is the condition of all civilized advance. Absent the division of labor, with its attendant specialization, we would not inhabit the utopia limned in the *Manifesto*[259] and the *Critique of the Gotha Programme*;[260] we would instead quickly descend into barbarism.

---

[255]"Freedom, Inequality, Primitivism, and the Division of Labor," in *Egalitarianism as a Revolt Against Nature*, pp. 247–303.

[256]*An Austrian Perspective on the History of Economic Thought*, 2 vols. (1995; Auburn, Ala.: Ludwig von Mises Institute, 2006).

[257]Karl Marx, *The Economic and Philosophic Manuscripts of 1844* (Moscow: Foreign Languages Publishing House, 1961).

[258]Karl Marx and Friedrich Engels, *The Communist Manifesto* (Long, 1848), close of chap. 2.

[259]Ibid.

[260]Karl Marx, *Critique of the Gotha Programme* (New York: International Publishers, 1938).

Why, then, do many intellectuals continue to claim that the division of labor dehumanizes?

In large part, Rothbard argues, these intellectuals have fallen victim to a myth popular in the Romantic Era. The Romantics conjured up primitive men who, untouched by the division of labor, lived in harmony with nature. Rothbard will have none of this. In a few well-chosen words, he excoriates Karl Polanyi, an influential panegyrist of the primitive: "This worship of the primitive permeates Polanyi's book, which at one point seriously applies the term 'noble savage' to the Kaffirs of South Africa."[261]

In an "Introduction" dated February 1991 to a reprint of the essay, he refines his critique even further. He notes, following M.H. Abrams, that the Romantic myth of primitivism rests upon a yet deeper layer of myth. According to the "emanationist" view, which has influenced both neo-Platonism and Gnosticism, creation is fundamentally evil. Human beings must be reabsorbed into the primitive oneness of all things. Rothbard sees this strange doctrine as "constituting a heretical and mystical underground in Western thought."[262]

It is clear that Rothbard views Romanticism in decidedly negative terms, at least so far as its impact on politics is concerned. He makes clear the nefarious consequences of Romanticism in the aforementioned article, "Left and Right: The Prospects for Liberty."[263] The exaltation of the primitive, which characterizes the Romantics, is by no means confined to the Left. Quite the contrary, it underlies apologies for what Rothbard terms the "Old Order" of feudalism and militarism. Both European conservatism and socialism reject the free market. Accordingly, Rothbard argues, a task of lovers of liberty is to oppose both these ideologies.

---

[261]"Freedom, Inequality, Primitivism, and the Division of Labor," in *Egalitarianism as a Revolt Against Nature*, note on p. 64.

[262]Ibid., p. 298.

[263]Reprinted in ibid., pp. 21–53.

In doing so, he maintains, libertarians must adopt a revolutionary strategy. Not for Rothbard is the path of compromise: all statist ideologies must be combated root-and-branch. He notes that
Lord Acton, long before Leon Trotsky, advocated "permanent revolution."[264]

Rothbard, incidentally, disconcerted American Romantic conservatives by arguing that Edmund Burke's early *Vindication of Natural Society*[265] was not a satire but a seriously intended defense of
anarchism. If Rothbard is right, the chief icon of the American tra-
ditionalists was once a libertarian. The article, "A Note on Burke's
Vindication of Natural Society," appeared in the *Journal of the History of Ideas*.[266] It aroused much controversy, but the eminent
Burke scholar Isaac Kramnick speaks highly of it in his *The Rage of
Edmund Burke*.[267]

Society, Rothbard has argued, rests on the division of labor.
Given the manifest advantages of peaceful cooperation that uses
human differences in abilities to the greatest extent possible, what
blocks human progress? Rothbard, in his essay "The Anatomy of
the State,"[268] identifies the chief obstacle to human betterment.
Unlike voluntary exchange, which by its nature benefits those who
freely choose to engage in it, the State rests on predation. Following Franz Oppenheimer and Albert Jay Nock, Rothbard contends
that the State cannot create wealth: it can only take from some and
give to others. Like them, he contrasts the "political means" with
"the economic means."

---

[264]Ibid., p. 29.

[265]Edmund Burke, *Vindication of Natural Society* (Indianapolis:
LibertyClassics, 1982).

[266]"A Note on Burke's Vindication of Natural Society," in *Journal of
the History of Ideas* (January 1958).

[267]Isaac Kramnick, *The Rage of Edmund Burke* (New York: Basic
Books, 1977).

[268]"The Anatomy of the State," in *Egalitarianism as a Revolt Against
Nature*, pp. 55–88.

If Rothbard is right, we now stand in no doubt as to our main obstacle in defending liberty: the Leviathan State. In "War, Peace, and the State,"[269] Rothbard narrows the target, in order to enable defenders of liberty to wage their struggle more effectively. One activity more than any other marks the State as the enemy of liberty, and it is here that supporters of liberty must concentrate their efforts.

The activity, of course, is waging war. Besides the death and destruction directly incident on war, nations engaging in armed conflict pay a heavy price in liberty. Accordingly, Rothbard calls for nations to engage in a strictly defensive foreign policy. Crusades "to make the world safe for democracy" stimulate him to opposition: how can the chief agency of predation, the State, serve as a means to secure freedom? In "National Liberation,"[270] however, he refuses to extend his condemnation of war to revolution. Often, revolutions manifest a drive against the State and merit support.

Unfortunately for the cause of liberty, political philosophers have not rushed to embrace Rothbard's revolutionary challenge to the foundations of their discipline. One of the characteristic objections mainstream theorists have to natural rights libertarianism goes like this: "Even if one concedes that self-ownership applies to rational adults, what is to be done with children? Surely the rights of these dependent human beings, and our duties toward them, cannot be encompassed within the confines of Rothbard's framework."

Rothbard was well aware of this objection, and in "Kid Lib,"[271] he offers a cogent response. He sensitively balances the rights of children, which increase as they become capable of exercising self-ownership, with the powers of parents to set rules for those living in their home and under their support.

---

[269]"War, Peace, and the State," in ibid, pp. 115–32.

[270]"National Liberation," in ibid, 195–98.

[271]"Kid Lib," in ibid, pp. 145–55.

Rothbard continually alternated between elaborations of principle and applications to particular issues. In "The Great Women's Liberation Issue: Setting It Straight,"[272] Rothbard applies a principle to which we have already made frequent reference. People differ in their abilities, a fact that egalitarians neglect at their peril. But do not men and women also differ in abilities? The unisex dreams of radical feminists contravene nature and must be rejected.

Rothbard's own stance on the women's movement characteristically stresses freedom.

> I do not go so far as the extreme male "sexists" who contend that women *should* confine themselves to the home and children and that any search for alternative careers is unnatural. On the other hand, I do not see much more support for the opposite contention that domestic-type women are violating *their* natures.[273]

Rothbard, like Nock, could speak of "our enemy, the State." But it does not follow that he viewed all anarchists with sympathy. Quite the contrary, in "Anarcho-Communism,"[274] Rothbard makes evident his distaste for anarchists who seek to combine opposition to the State with communism. Often the advocates of this position straightforwardly embrace irrationalism. Norman O. Brown, a Freudian classicist much in favor with the New Left, contended that socialists, in the face of Mises's proof that a socialist system cannot calculate, should abandon economic calculation for a world of polymorphous perversity.

Like his Marxist adversaries, Rothbard stressed the unity of theory and practice: philosophy is a guide to action. In "Why Be

---

[272]"The Great Women's Liberation Issue: Setting It Straight," in ibid., pp. 157–73.

[273]Ibid., pp. 162–63; emphasis in the original.

[274]"Anarcho-Communism," in ibid., pp. 199–204.

Libertarian?"[275] he asks the most basic question of all: why should libertarian theorizing matter to us? The answer cannot be found, he contends, in the narrow pursuit of individual advantage. Only the love of justice suffices.

In an effort to widen the influence of libertarian thought in the academic world, Rothbard founded the *Journal of Libertarian Studies* in 1977. The journal began auspiciously with a symposium on Robert Nozick's *Anarchy, State, and Utopia*. Down to the present, it has remained the most important journal hospitable to libertarian ideas.

Rothbard established in 1987 another journal, the *Review of Austrian Economics*, to provide a scholarly venue for economists and others interested in Austrian theory. It too is the key journal in its area of specialty. It has continued to the present, after 1997 under the new name *Quarterly Journal of Austrian Economics*.

In his comments on current events, Rothbard displayed an amazing ability to digest vast quantities of information on whatever subject interested him. Whether, e.g., the question was competing factions in Afghanistan or the sources of investment in oil in the Middle East, he would always have the relevant data at his command. A sample of his columns, taken from the *Rothbard-Rockwell Report*, is available in *The Irrepressible Rothbard*.[276]

This indispensable collection contains a key statement of Rothbard's views on foreign policy, which explain in more detail the rationale for the noninterventionist policy we have already seen he favors. In a few paragraphs, he eviscerates the prevailing doctrine of twentieth-century American foreign policy.

According to the accepted picture, totalitarian powers twice threatened America during the twentieth century. Germany, under the maniacal leadership of Hitler, aimed at world conquest. After

---

[275]"Why Be Libertarian?" in ibid., pp. 239–45.

[276]Llewellyn H., Rockwell, Jr., ed., *The Irrepressible Rothbard* (Auburn, Ala.: Mises Institute, 2000).

the United States and her allies succeeded in halting the Nazis, a new menace demanded attention.

One of our allies in World War II, the Soviet Union, was itself a militantly expansionist state; it had to be contained during the protracted Cold War. At various times during the Cold War, and continuing after it to the present, hostile and aggressive dictators presented America with problems. Saddam Hussein ranks as perhaps the most notorious of these tyrants.

The accepted picture draws a lesson from all these events. An aggressive power, almost always led by a dictator, must be dealt with as one would handle a neighborhood bully. Only firm dealings with the dictator can stave off war.

Since bullies generally are cowards, dictators will back down if directly challenged. The Munich Conference, September 29 and 30, 1938, perfectly illustrates how not to handle a dictator. Britain and France appeased Hitler; the result was war one year later. Had Britain and France acted when Hitler remilitarized the Rhineland in 1936, the Nazis could have been overthrown virtually without cost.

Rothbard at once locates the fallacy in this oft-repeated line of thought.

> Answer me this, war hawks: when, in history, when did one State, faced with belligerent, ultra-tough ultimatums by another, when did that one State ever give up and in effect surrender—before any war was fought? When?[277]

Rothbard's rhetorical question rests upon a simple point of psychology. The supposed "bully" cannot surrender to an ultimatum lest he be overthrown.

> No head of State with any pride or self-respect, or who wishes to keep the respect of his citizens, will surrender to such an ultimatum.[278]

---

[277]Ibid., p. 170.

[278]Ibid., p. 170.

The Gulf War perfectly illustrates Rothbard's contention. Faced with an overwhelming show of force, Saddam Hussein did not back down. Rothbard's generalization explains Saddam's seemingly irrational response.

But have we not forgotten something? What about World War II? Does not the failure to confront Hitler over Czechoslovakia in 1938 prove conclusively the thesis of the antiappeasers? Rothbard's response illustrates his ability to counter an opposing argument at its strongest point.

> Neither was World War II in Europe a case where toughness worked. On the contrary, Hitler disregarded the English guarantee to Poland that brought England and France into the German-Polish war in September 1939.[279]

A belligerent foreign policy, then, will most likely lead to the wars it professes to deter. But who urges us toward this course? Rothbard arraigns the social democrats and their successors, the neoconservatives. These he accuses of support for statism at home and war abroad.

Rothbard tersely sums up the credo of social democracy in this way:

> on all crucial issues, social democrats stand against liberty and tradition, and in favor of statism and Big Government. They are more dangerous in the long run than the communists not simply because they have endured, but also because their program and their rhetorical appeals are far more insidious, since they claim to combine socialism with the appealing virtues of "democracy" and freedom of inquiry.[280]

For Rothbard, the State always ranks as the principal enemy. The battle against the "massive welfare-warfare State" to him was

---

[279]Ibid.
[280]Ibid., p. 23.

no mere clash of abstractions. Quite the contrary, he aimed at particular targets who embodied the statist doctrines he abhorred. Sidney Hook occupied a place near the summit of his intellectual foes. A precocious communist theorist in the 1920s, Hook found the Soviet Union insufficiently revolutionary and soon beat the drums for militant anticommunism, though of a distinctly socialist cast. Throughout his long life, he called for war, first against Nazi Germany and then against Stalin and his successors. According to Rothbard, "[o]ne's attitude toward Sidney Hook . . . provides a convenient litmus test on whether someone is a genuine conservative, a paleo, or some form of neo."[281]

The struggle against the State needed to be waged on many fronts. Rothbard saw a disturbing trend among certain left-libertarians. Although libertarianism quintessentially opposes state power, some doctrinal deviants allowed the enemy to enter through the back door.

They did so by holding that public agencies must observe rules of nondiscriminatory treatment. These rules have nothing to do with the free market, but everything to do with the slogans of the contemporary Left. Rothbard expertly locates the central fallacy in the argument of the libertarian heretics. Since nearly everything today partakes to a degree of the State, the new doctrine leads to total government control.

Rothbard states his point with characteristic panache:

> But not only literal government operations are subject to this egalitarian doctrine. It also applies to any activities which are tarred with the public brush, with the use, for example, of government streets, or any acceptance of taxpayer funds. . . . sometimes, libertarians fall back on the angry argument that, nowadays, you can't really distinguish between "public" and "private" anyway.[282]

---

[281]Ibid., p. 25.
[282]Ibid., p. 103.

Left-libertarianism is of course not for Rothbard the main problem that faces America: we confront an all out statist attack on liberty, conducted by the "opinion leaders" in academia and elsewhere. How has this assault managed to do so well? Rothbard's answer exposes the philosophical roots of the problem. No longer does the academic elite believe in objective morality, grasped by right reason. Lacking a rational basis for moral values, our supposed intellectual leaders readily fall prey to statist fallacy.

The beginning stage of nihilism, Rothbard maintains, occurred in art.

> First, the left-liberals preached *l'art pour l'art* in aesthetics, and as a corollary, in ethics, trumpeted the new view that there is no such thing as a revealed or objective ethics, that all ethics are "subjective," that all of life's choices are only personal, emotive "preferences."[283]

Rothbard strongly opposed modern art, and he thought highly of the critical account of it in the book by the Austrian art historian Hans Sedlmayr, *Art in Crisis: The Lost Center*.[284]

The denial of objective standards in the name of freedom has led to death and destruction. Rothbard maintains that ethical nihilism results in the overthrow of the most basic human rights, including the right not to be murdered. He has not the slightest sympathy for the rampant pro-euthanasia movement.

> No, the mask is off, and Doctor Assisted Death and Mr. Liberal Death With Dignity, and all the rest of the crew turn out to be Doctor and Mister Murder. Watch out Mr. And Mrs. America: liberal humanists, lay and medical, are . . . out to kill you.[285]

---

[283]Ibid., p. 296.

[284]Hans Sedlmayr, *Art in Crisis: The Lost Center* (London: Hollis and Carter, 1959).

[285]Llewellyn H. Rockwell, Jr., ed., *The Irrepressible Rothbard*, p. 303.

What can be done to combat statism and nihilism? Rothbard views populism with great sympathy. As so often in his work, he rethought and deepened his position. He determined that the common libertarian strategy of looking to the courts to enforce rights was mistaken.

Even in cases in which courts enforce the "correct" position, the imperatives of states' rights and local control should not be overturned. Thus, Rothbard favored a "pro-choice" position on abortion. But he was loath to have courts enforce abortion rights on recalcitrant states.

"No, libertarians should no longer be complacent about centralization and national jurisdiction—the equivalent," he writes,

> of foreign intervention or of reaching for global dictatorship. Kansans henceforth should take their chances in Kansas; Nevadans in Nevada, etc. And if women find that abortion clinics are not defended in Kansas, they can travel to New York or Nevada.[286]

Although Rothbard found great merit in populism, he did not defend the movement uncritically. He saw danger in leftist populism; a true populist movement must not abandon the free market in favor of crackpot panaceas. In one of the last articles he wrote, he warned Pat Buchanan against this danger:

> In this murky and volatile situation, the important thing for us paleo-populists is that we find a candidate as soon as possible who will lead and develop the cause and the movement of right-wing populism, to raise the standard of the Old, free, decentralized, and strictly limited Republic.[287]

Another journal that he founded, *The Libertarian Forum*, provides his topical comments for the period 1969–1984. He presented a comprehensive popular account of libertarianism in *For A*

---

[286]Ibid., p. 306.
[287]Ibid., p. 141.

New Liberty (1973).[288] He worked actively for many years as a leading member of the Libertarian Party. In an effort to resist the abandonment of libertarian principles by factions within that party, he led the Radical Caucus. Justin Raimondo has discussed Rothbard's political activities in great detail in his *Enemy of the State: The Life of Murray N. Rothbard*.[289] Raimondo was a member of the Radical Caucus and writes from the perspective of an activist in sympathy with Rothbard. At the end of the 1980s, Rothbard left the Libertarian Party.

Some professed to find a contradiction in Rothbard's political activities. He often criticized other libertarians for deviating from the correct "line"; yet he himself sought alliances with divergent groups, both on the Left and the Right. There is in fact no contradiction here: Rothbard held libertarians to a much stricter standard than outsiders. For those within the fold, doctrinal orthodoxy was a must; but alliances with outsiders were another matter. Here tactics were all important, and a general agreement on principles was neither required nor expected.

ROTHBARD ON CURRENT ECONOMIC ISSUES

He offered comments on current economic issues in *The Free Market*, published by the Ludwig von Mises Institute; and a collection of his columns from 1982 to 1995 is available in *Making Economic Sense*.[290]

---

[288]*For A New Liberty: The Libertarian Manifesto*, 2nd ed. (1973; Auburn, Ala.: Ludwig von Mises Institute, 2006).

[289]Justin Raimondo, *Enemy of the State: The Life of Murray N. Rothbard* (New York: Prometheus Books, 2000).

[290]*Making Economic Sense*, 2nd ed. (Auburn, Ala.: Ludwig von Mises Institute, 2006).

Many economists have noted that in a free market, consumers have much greater freedom of choice than in an economy run by government coercion. But here a misstep threatens. Because consumers have greater choice in a free market, it is easy to jump to the conclusion that whatever promotes choice is a free market measure. Thus, Milton Friedman, in some circles "the very essence of a modern major general" of free market forces, has supported vouchers so that parents can send their children to the schools they choose for them.

Rothbard at once penetrates to the heart of the matter in his analysis.

> [B]y fatuously focusing on potential "choice," the voucher revolutionaries forget that expanding the "choices" of poor parents by giving them more taxpayer money also *restricts* the "choices" of the suburban parents and private-school parents from having the sort of education that *they* want for their kids.[291]

The focus, he argues, should not be on the abstract notion of "choice" but on money and income. The person who earns more money necessarily has more "choices" on how to spend that money. A simple point: a free market society rests on a system of property rights, not on a futile effort to maximize choices, of whatever sort. Yet who before Rothbard saw the point so clearly and so well?

Rothbard was ever alert to mistaken arguments for capitalism that, in an effort to be value free, lack a sound foundation in ethical theory. We have earlier seen his criticism of the Pareto criterion as a welfare ideal: in an article included here, he brilliantly illustrates how the criterion operates in practice.

> A grotesque example of a "free-market" "expert" on efficiency slightly moderating totalitarianism was the proposal of the anti-population fanatic and distinguished economist . . . Kenneth E. Boulding. Boulding proposed the typical

---

[291]Ibid., p. 159; emphasis in the original.

"reform" of an economist. Instead of forcing every woman to be sterilized after having two babies, the government would issue each woman . . . two baby-rights.[292]

The mother could have two babies; if she wanted more, she could purchase baby rights from a woman who wanted to trade hers in. "[I]f we start from the original ZPG [Zero Population Growth] plan," Rothbard comments, "and we introduce the Boulding plan, wouldn't everyone be better off, and the requirements of 'Pareto superiority' therefore obtain?"[293]

If the key to a free society is not to be found in standard welfare economics, neither is resort to that contemporary shibboleth, democracy, sufficient. The mere fact that a majority of a society supports some measure tells us very little about that measure's desirability:

> What, in fact, is so great about democracy? Democracy is scarcely a virtue in itself, much less an overriding one, and not nearly as important as liberty, property rights, a free market, or strictly limited government. Democracy is simply a process, a means of selecting government rulers and policies. It has but one virtue, but this can indeed be an important one: it provides a peaceful means for the triumph of the popular will.[294]

With Rothbard, one can rarely predict what is coming next. No matter how carefully one thinks one has grasped his thought, he was always several steps ahead. Thus, what follows from the passage just quoted? One might think that, given his view of democracy, he would call for us sharply to de-emphasize democratic reforms. Quite the contrary, he demands more democracy.

---

[292]Ibid., p. 152.

[293]Ibid.

[294]Ibid., p. 487; the essay, "The November Revolution . . . And What To Do About It," from which this quotation comes was a Confidential Memo that was made available to the public for the first time in *Making Economic Sense*.

It does not at all follow from the fact that democracy is theoretically inessential that moves in a democratic direction cannot be the order of the day. Rothbard was especially concerned to strip from the judiciary its power to overturn popularly supported initiatives. In a highhanded way, our judicial lords and masters find in the Constitution the leftist values they have imposed on that document. Rothbard would have none of this: he proposed measures that would "effectively crush the power of the Supreme Court."[295]

Rothbard, it is sufficiently clear, was no conventional economist. His economic analysis was always embedded within a careful account of politics and ethics. Thus, many economists, when considering Nafta [North American Free Trade Agreement], saw only that some tariffs would by its terms be lowered. Was this not a move toward free trade that deserved the support of libertarians?

Rothbard's analysis penetrates much deeper.

> The worst aspects of Nafta are the Clintonian side agreements, which have converted an unfortunate Bush [I] treaty into a horror of international statism. We have the side agreements to thank for the supra-national Commissions and their coming "upward harmonization." The side agreements also push the foreign aid aspect of the establishment's "free trade hoax."[296]

He also noted another problem with Nafta, which escaped the attention of most commentators: "Nafta is called a trade agreement so it can avoid the constitutional requirement of approval by two-thirds of the Senate."[297]

Rothbard's treatment of the politics of economic issues covers a vast field, but one theme stands uppermost. Whatever advances the power of the state is for him a deadly danger. And even worse than an increase in the power of a single state was the rise of an imperial power that sought world domination.

---

[295]Ibid., p. 490.

[296]Ibid., p. 374.

[297]Ibid., p. 371.

Here he saw a prime danger of Nafta, a vital step to a New World Order. Politically, it suggests that the United States is "totally committed" to a form of global government. Economically, it means not free trade but a "managed, cartelized trade and production, the economy to be governed by an oligarchic ruling coalition of Big Government, Big Business, and Big Intellectuals/Big Media."[298]

ROTHBARD'S LAST SCHOLARLY TRIUMPH

One last academic triumph remained for Rothbard, though sadly it appeared only after his death. In two massive volumes, *Economic Thought Before Adam Smith* and *Classical Economics*[299] he presented a minutely detailed and erudite account of the history of economic theory. For Rothbard, the history of economics has an unusually broad scope. To him it includes not only economic theory but virtually all of intellectual history as well. He advances definite and well thought out interpretations of major historical controversies.

As an example, Machiavelli was in his view a "preacher of evil"—not for him the fashionable portrayal of the Florentine as the founder of value-free political science. With characteristic acuity, Rothbard asks:

> Who in the history of the world, after all, and outside a Dr. Fu Manchu novel, has actually lauded evil *per se* and counselled evil and vice at every step of life's way? Preaching evil is to counsel precisely as Machiavelli has done: be good so long as goodness doesn't get in the way of something you

---

[298]Ibid., p. 377.

[299]*An Austrian Perspective on the History of Economic Thought*, vol. 1: *Economic Thought Before Adam Smith*, and vol. 2: *Classical Economics* (Cheltenham, U.K.: Edward Elgar, 1995).

want, in the case of the ruler that something being the main-
tenance and expansion of power.[300]

He concludes his discussion with a stinging rebuke to modern
political scientists, who "eschew moral principles as being 'unscientific' and therefore outside their sphere of interest."[301]

Rothbard firmly rejects the thesis of Max Weber, according to
which the "inner-wordly asceticism" that Calvinism encouraged
played a key role in the rise of capitalism. Rothbard counters that
capitalism began long before Calvin; and the stress on "God and
profit" that Weber found distinctively Protestant was present in
the Catholic Middle Ages.

For the Weber thesis, Rothbard substitutes another contrast
between Catholics and Protestants, here following Emil Kauder.
The Calvinist stress on the calling led to emphasis on work and
saving and distrust of consumption: Catholic Europe, following
the Aristotelian and scholastic tradition, found nothing wrong with
consumption. This difference led to a crucial split in the growth of
economics, between utility and cost-of-production theories of
price.

In an insightful passage, Rothbard sets aside oceans of misin-
terpretation about the quarrel between the Ancients and the Mod-
erns.

> The pitting of "tradition" vs. "modernity" is largely an artifi-
> cial antithesis. "Moderns" like Locke or perhaps even
> Hobbes may have been individualists and "right-thinkers,"
> but they were also steeped in scholasticism and natural
> law.[302]

Further, on the same page he strikes at another theory of vast
but unmerited influence:

---

[300]*Economic Thought Before Adam Smith*, p. 190.
[301]Ibid., p. 192.
[302]Ibid., pp. 313–14.

> Neither are John Pocock and his followers convincing in try-
> ing to posit an artificial distinction and clash between the lib-
> ertarian concerns of Locke or his later followers on the one
> hand, and devotion to "classical virtue" on the other . . . why
> can't libertarians and opposers of government intervention
> *also* oppose government "corruption" and extravagance?
> Indeed, the two generally go together.[303]

Rothbard firmly opposes the Whig view of the history of economics, in which "later" is inevitably "better," thus rendering the
study of the past unnecessary. In his view, much of the history of
economics consists of wrong turnings; and volume I ends with a
tale of decline. Yet, paradoxically, Rothbard's own method is in
another way Whiggish itself. He has his own firmly held positions
on correct economic theory, based on his adherence to the tenets
of the Austrian School. He accordingly is anxious to see how various figures anticipate key Austrian views or, on the contrary, pursue blind alleys.

The dominant theme in Rothbard's appraisal of economics is
the nature of value. Economic actors, endeavoring to better their
own positions, guide themselves by their subjective appraisals of
goods and services. The pursuit of an "objective" measure of value
is futile; what influence can such an alleged criterion have, unless
it is reflected in the minds of economic agents?

Rothbard especially emphasizes, in this connection, the so-
called paradox of value. How can it be that water costs little or
nothing while diamonds are extraordinarily expensive? Life cannot
exist without the former, while the latter are the merest luxuries.
Does not this paradox show that goods do not exchange according
to their subjective values? The answer, fully developed by the Austrian School, depends on the fact that subjective appraisals of particular units of a good, not the supposed value of the whole stock
of the good, determine price. Since water is abundant and diamonds are scarce, there is no anomaly at all in the greater price of
the latter.

---

[303]Ibid., p. 314.

Rothbard never fails to praise those who reach or approach this insight. The scholastics fare especially well: Pierre de Jean Olivi, e.g., realized that the

> important factor in determining price is *complacibilitas*, or subjective utility, the subjective desirability of a product to the individual consumers. . . . [u]tility, in the determination of price, is relative to supply and not absolute.[304]

He lauds Jean Buridan for extending the subjective utility analysis to money.

A key corollary of the subjectivist position is that an exchange does not consist of an equality: each party values more highly what he obtains than what he surrenders. Those who miss this point elicit a protest from Rothbard. Aristotle, whom he much admires as a philosopher, does not escape censure:

> Aristotle's famous discussion of reciprocity in exchange in Book V of his *Nicomachean Ethics* is a prime example of descent into gibberish. Aristotle talks of a builder exchanging a house for the shoes produced by a shoemaker. He then writes: "The number of shoes exchanged for a house must therefore correspond to the ratio of builder to shoemaker. . . ." Eh? How can there possibly be a ratio of "builder" to "shoemaker"?[305]

Those who knew Murray Rothbard can almost hear him asking this.

The subjectivist insight by no means died with the close of the Middle Ages. On the contrary, the School of Salamanca upheld it in the sixteenth century; and in the eighteenth, Cantillon and Turgot considerably extended it. But the path of economics was not one of continual progress. Theory suffered a major setback through the work of one of Rothbard's main antiheroes, Adam Smith.

---

[304]Ibid., p. 61.
[305]Ibid., p. 16.

Far from being the founder of economics, Smith in the eyes of Rothbard was almost its gravedigger. Although Smith in his classroom lectures solved the paradox of value in standard subjectivist fashion, "in the *Wealth of Nations*, for some bizarre reason, all this drops out and falls away."[306] Smith threw out subjective utility and instead attempted to explain price through labor cost. Because of Smith's mistake, the "great tradition [of subjectivism] gets poured down the Orwellian memory hole."[307]

Rothbard also diverges from the mainstream interpretation of Smith in his account of the "invisible hand." He views this as expressive of Smith's Calvinist belief in Divine Providence; he does not regard the concept as an important analytical tool.

The second volume, *Classical Economics*, continues to emphasize the struggle between subjectivists and their antagonists. Another central theme emerges in the volume's initial chapter: "J.B. Say: the French Tradition in Smithian Clothing." Jean-Baptiste Say, far from being a mere popularizer of Adam Smith, "was the first economist to think deeply about the proper methodology of his discipline, and to base his work, as far as he could, upon that methodology."[308]

And what is the procedure that Say advocated? One starts from certain "general facts" that are incontestably known to be true. From these, the economist reasons deductively. Since the beginning axioms are true, whatever is validly deduced from them also is true. Here, in brief compass Say discovered the praxeological method that came to full fruition in the work of Mises and Rothbard himself.

To understand praxeology, a key point about the initial axioms must be kept in mind. The starting points are common sense, "obvious" truths, e.g., that people engage in exchange in order to

---

[306]Ibid., p. 449.
[307]Ibid., p. 450.
[308]*Classical Economics*, p. 12.

benefit themselves. The economist should not begin from over-simplified hypotheses about the economy as a whole, chosen because convenient for mathematical manipulation. Adoption of the wrong method was the besetting vice of David Ricardo, the main impediment, in Rothbard's view, to the development of economics in the nineteenth century.

This conflict of method had a fundamental effect on the content of Say's and Ricardo's economics. Say began from the individual in action, the subject of the common sense propositions he took to be axiomatic. Thus, Say placed great emphasis on the entrepreneur. One cannot assume that the economy automatically adjusts itself: only by the foresight of those able and willing to take risks can production be allocated efficiently. "It seems to us that Say is foursquare in the Cantillon-Turgot tradition of the entrepreneur as forecaster and risk-bearer."[309]

Again, Say's stress on the individual underlies his analysis of taxation, which Rothbard rates among his greatest contributions. Some, including notoriously Adam Smith, consider taxes a way to benefit the public; but Say would have nothing to do with such nonsense. Taxation, in essence, is theft; the government forcibly seizes property from its rightful owners. If the powers-that-be then condescend to spend some of their ill-gotten gains for the "public benefit," they are in reality purchasing people's goods with the people's own money. Taxation, accordingly, should be as low as possible: the search of Smith and his followers for "canons of justice" in taxation must be rejected. Rothbard characteristically adds: why have any taxes at all?

When we turn to Rothbard on Ricardo, the atmosphere is entirely different. Once again, he reverses conventional opinion. Say was not a popularizer, but a great economist; likewise contrary to the prevailing view, Ricardo was not the first truly scientific economist. His much-praised logic is "verbal mathematics" that fundamentally misconceives economics.

---

[309]Ibid., p. 26.

> Ricardo was stuck with a hopeless problem: he had four vari-
> ables, but only one equation with which to solve them:
>
> Total output (or income) = rent + profit + wages
>
> To solve, or rather pretend to solve, this equation, Ricardo
> had to "determine" one or more of these entities from out-
> side his equation, and in such a way as to leave others as resid-
> uals.[310]

Rothbard explains with crystal clarity the path by which
Ricardo sought to escape. He simply held fixed as many of his variables as he could: by oversimplified assumptions, he could "solve"
his equations. In particular, he adopted a theory of rent based on
differential productivity, which Rothbard neatly skewers; and he
made price largely a function of the quantity of labor time embodied in a commodity's production.

Ricardo's labor theory of value had a consequence that would
no doubt have shocked its author. It paved the way for Marxism.

> Marx found a crucial key to this mechanism [by which the
> capitalist class would be expropriated] in Ricardo's labour
> theory of value, and in the Ricardian socialist thesis that
> labour is the sole determinant of value, with capital's share, or
> profits, being the "surplus value" extracted by the capitalist
> from labour's created product.[311]

And with his stress on the Ricardian roots of Marxism, Rothbard
begins a devastating assault on "scientific socialism," the like of
which has not been seen since Böhm-Bawerk.

As Rothbard notes, Marx's economics falls into error from the
start. Marx assumed that in an exchange, the commodities traded
have equal value. Moreover, he took this postulated equality in a
very strong sense: both of the goods must be identical to some
third thing. This, by spurious reasoning that Rothbard deftly
exposes, he claimed could only be labor.

---

[310]Ibid., p. 82.
[311]Ibid., p. 409.

But the flaw in Marx's derivation does not lie only in the details of his argument. A leitmotif of Rothbard's work is that, as previously mentioned, an exchange consists not of an equality, but rather of a double inequality. Marx's whole edifice thus rests on a spurious assumption, and the three volumes of *Das Kapital*[312] constitute an elaborate attempt to conjure a solution to a nonexistent problem.

But the difficulties of Marxist economics are not confined to its starting point. Rothbard acutely notes that Marx's theory of wage determination really applies not to capitalism but to slavery:

> Oddly, neither Marx nor his critics ever realized that there is one place in the economy where the Marxist theory of exploitation and surplus *does* apply: not to the capitalist-worker relation in the market, but to the relation of master and slave under slavery. Since the masters own the slaves, they indeed only pay them their subsistence wage: enough to live on and reproduce, while the masters pocket the surplus of the slaves' marginal product over their cost of subsistence.[313]

Rothbard does not confine his assault on Marxism to an exposure of its economic fallacies. Behind the economics of Marxism, he finds a heretical religious myth, the goal of which is the "obliteration of the individual through 'reunion' with God, the One, and the ending of cosmic 'alienation,' at least on the level of each individual."[314]

One might at first think that abstruse theosophical speculations that date back to Plotinus have little to do with Marxism. But Rothbard convincingly shows that Marx, through the intermediary of Hegel, presented a secularized version of this witches' brew in the guise of "scientific socialism." In the course of doing so, Rothbard makes Hegel's philosophy seem amusing; his remarks on the

---

[312]Karl Marx, *Das Kapital* (New York: E.P. Dutton, 1962).

[313]*Classical Economics*, p. 393; emphasis in the original.

[314]Ibid., p. 351.

"cosmic blob" are worthy of H.L. Mencken (who was, incidentally, one of Rothbard's favorite authors). Rothbard's analysis of Marx's philosophy reinforces the pioneering investigations of Eric Voegelin; this parallel between the conclusions of these two great scholars is all the more remarkable in that Rothbard, though familiar with Voegelin, was not deeply influenced by him.[315]

In his discussion of utilitarianism, Rothbard's philosophical turn of mind is evident. He notes that according to that system, reason

> is only a hand-maiden, a slave to the passions. . . . But what, then, is to be done about the fact that most people decide about their ends by ethical principles, which cannot be considered reducible to an original personal emotion?[316]

Rothbard has here rediscovered an objection to utilitarianism raised by Archbishop Whately: how can utilitarianism accommodate preferences based on competing ethical systems? John Stuart Mill, though familiar with the objection, never answered it in a convincing way.

Rothbard viewed Mill with contempt, and his mordant portrayal of him is one of the highlights of the book:

> John Stuart was the quintessence of soft rather than hardcore, a woolly minded man of mush in striking contrast to his steel-edged father [James Mill]. . . . John [Stuart] Mill's enormous popularity and stature in the British intellectual world was partially due to his very mush-headedness.[317]

Rothbard's two volumes, which he unfortunately did not live to see published, are a monument of twentieth-century scholarship. Roger Backhouse, an eminent historian of economic thought, notes in his review that

---

[315]Also illuminating in this regard is Cyril O'Regan's *The Heterodox Hegel* (New York: SUNY Press, 1994).

[316]*Classical Economics*, p. 57.

[317]Ibid., p. 277.

the range of authors discussed is immense. Rothbard clearly makes the point that economics is the product of communities of scholars, not simply a small group of pioneering thinkers . . . his reading is vast, and there is much to be learned from him.[318]

Backhouse disagrees with Rothbard's Austrian perspective; nevertheless, he concludes that "it is nonetheless, an exciting, even brilliant, book."[319]

FOLLOWERS AND INFLUENCE

He taught at Brooklyn Polytechnic Institute from the mid-1960s to the mid-1980s; from 1986 to his death on January 7, 1995, he was S.J. Hall Distinguished Professor of Economics at the University of Nevada, Las Vegas.

Rothbard was closely associated with the Ludwig von Mises Institute from its founding in 1982 by Llewellyn H. Rockwell, Jr. This organization became the main vehicle for the promotion of his ideas, and he served as its Academic Vice-President. Most of the academics who have endeavored to continue Rothbard's work have been associated with the Mises Institute. Among economists, Joseph T. Salerno has carried out important research on the history of the Austrian School. He has made clear the distinctive nature of the economics of Mises and Rothbard and has also done pioneering work on nineteenth-century bullionist economists. Hans-Hermann Hoppe has extended Rothbard's work in political philosophy with a much-discussed argument for libertarian rights that Rothbard admired. Peter G. Klein has creatively applied Misesian and Rothbardian insights to industrial organization. Walter Block, the most prolific of Rothbard's followers, has, among many

---

[318]*History of Economic Thought Newsletter* 56 (Summer, 1996): 20.
[319]*Classical Economics*, p. 21.

other contributions, a notable series of articles criticizing the Coase theorem.[320] Jörg Guido Hülsmann has written major papers on error cycles, counterfactuals in economic theory, and the interest rate. Jeffrey Herbener has been (along with Salerno and Hoppe) a major contributor to the debate on the socialist calculation argument. Following Rothbard, these authors contend that Mises's argument differs from Hayek's: Mises's contention that a socialist economy could not calculate is not an argument that the planners lack the means to handle too much information or to handle "tacit knowledge." Rather, Mises's point concerns the impossibility of calculation without a system of market prices. Herbener has also done important work on welfare economics, in the tradition of Rothbard's "Toward a Reconstruction of Utility and Welfare Economics."

In other disciplines, two of Rothbard's closest friends merit special mention, the intellectual historians Ralph Raico and Ronald Hamowy. Both were members of the Circle Bastiat, a group of Rothbard's disciples that met in his apartment in New York during the 1950s.[321] Raico has written a history of German classical liberalism, as well as notable essays on World War I and on Winston Churchill.[322] Hamowy has edited a major scholarly edition of

---

[320]Rothbard anticipated some of Block's concerns about Coase. He noted that Coase "reveals grave collectivist distortions in his thinking." Coase would allow regulation to prevent acts that reduce competition, but "since the State can and has defined almost any act as reducing competition, this opens the gates for tyranny." Letter to Kenneth Templeton, July 16, 1957; Rothbard Papers.

[321]The Circle Bastiat consisted of: Murray Rothbard, Ralph Raico, Ronald Hamowy, George Reisman, Leonard Liggio, and Robert Hessen.

[322]Ralph Raico, *German Liberalism: Die Partei der Freiheit: Studien zur Geschichte des deutschen Liberalismus* (Stuttgart: Lucius & Lucius, 1999) and *Classical Liberalism: Historical Essays in Political Economy* (London: Routledge, forthcoming). Two notable essays are found in *The Costs of War*, Denson, ed., "World War I: The Turning Point" and "Rethinking Churchill."

Cato's Letters.[323] Also worthy of note is Llewellyn H. Rockwell, Jr.'s *Speaking of Liberty,*[324] a collection of essays which applies the insights of Mises and Rothbard to contemporary issues.

Many besides Rothbard's acknowledged followers have been influenced by him, but one striking example must here suffice. One of the most influential books of twentieth-century American philosophy has been Robert Nozick's *Anarchy, State, and Utopia.* Nozick remarks that it "was a long conversation about six years ago (i.e., in 1968) with Murray Rothbard that stimulated my interest in individualist anarchist theory." The entire first part of Nozick's book is an attempt to come to terms with Rothbard's argument and might have been entitled "Why I Am Not a Rothbardian."

The "indispensable framework" of life and work of this creative genius and polymath was his beloved wife, JoAnn Rothbard. His combination of scholarly achievement and engaged advocacy on behalf of freedom is unmatched. One can imagine what position in the academic world his immense talents would have secured for him had he been willing to adopt a political position more popular among his fellow economists; but he always stood by his beliefs above all else. He could say of himself, like Browning's *Paracelsus,*

> But after, they will know me. If I stoop
> Into a dark tremendous sea of cloud,
> It is but for a time; I press God's lamp
> Close to my breast; its splendour, soon or late,
> Will pierce the gloom: I shall emerge one day.[325]

---

[323]Ronald Hamowy, ed., *Cato's Letters or Essays on Liberty, Civil and Religious, and Other Important Subjects* (Indianapolis: Liberty Fund, 1995).

[324]Llewellyn H. Rockwell, Jr., ed., *Speaking of Liberty* (Auburn, Ala.: Ludwig von Mises Institute, 2003).

[325]Robert Browning, *Paracelsus,* Part V.

MURRAY N. ROTHBARD
CHRONOLOGICAL BIBLIOGRAPHY
(1949–1995)

1949

Review of *A Mencken Chrestomathy*, by H.L. Mencken. *analysis* (August 1949): 4.

Review of *The Road Ahead*, by John T. Flynn. *analysis* (December 1949): 4.

Review of *Nineteen Eighty-Four*, by George Orwell. "Our Future." *analysis* (September 1949): 4.

1950

Review of *Pioneers of American Freedom*, by Rudolf Rocker. *analysis* (January 1950): 4.

"Not Worth A Continental." *Faith and Freedom* (February 1950): 9–10.

"The Edict of Diocletian." *Faith and Freedom* (March 1950): 11.

Review of *Human Action*, by Ludwig von Mises. *analysis* (May 1950): 4.

Review of *Human Action*, by Ludwig von Mises. *Faith and Freedom* (September 1950): 14–15.

1951

SCHOLARLY ARTICLES AND CHAPTERS IN BOOKS:

"Mises's *Human Action*: Comment." *American Economic Review* (March 1951).

"Praxeology: Reply to Mr. Schuller." *American Economic Review* (December 1951).

OTHER:

"Well Labeled." Correspondence to *analysis* (January 1951): 4.

"Jefferson's Philosophy." *Faith and Freedom* (March 1951): 10–12.

"The Root of Old Hickory." *Faith and Freedom* (May 1951): 11–12.

1954

"The Real Aggressor." *Faith and Freedom* (April 1954): 22–27; under the pseudonym Aubrey Herbert. Reprinted in Rothbard and Jereme Tuccille, eds., *Left and Right: Selected Essays*. New York: Arno Press, 1972.

"There's No Middle Ground." *Faith and Freedom* (June 1954): 24–27; under the pseudonym Aubrey Herbert.

1955

Review of *Fabianism in the Political Life of Great Britain*, by Margaret M. McCarran. *Freeman* (April 1955): 447; under the pseudonym Aubrey Herbert.

"Fight For Formosa Or Not?" Part I. *Faith and Freedom* (May 1955): 7, 9; under the pseudonym Aubrey Herbert.

"Fight For Formosa Or Not?" Part II. *Faith and Freedom* (June 1955): 19, 21; under the pseudonym Aubrey Herbert.)

"The Ownership and Control of Water." *Ideas on Liberty* 3 (November 1955): 82–87; written anonymously.

"The Railroads of France." *Ideas On Liberty* (September 1955): 42–43.

1956

Scholarly Articles & Chapters in Books:

"Toward a Reconstruction of Utility and Welfare Economics." Mary Sennholz, ed., *On Freedom and Free Enterprise: Essays in Honor of Ludwig von Mises*. Princeton, N.J.: D. Van Nostrand, 1956, pp. 224–62. Reprinted as Occasional Paper Series #3. New York: Center for Libertarian Studies, 1977. Translated in French as "Vers une reconstruction de la théorie de l'utilité et du bien-être" by François Guillaumat in *Economistes et charlatans*. Paris: Les Belles Lettres, 1991, pp. 97–161. Reprinted in *The Logic of Action One: Method, Money, and the Austrian School*. Cheltenham, U.K.: Edward Elgar, 1997, pp. 211–54. Reprinted and expanded as *Economic Controversies*. Auburn, Ala.: Ludwig von Mises Institute, 2007.

Other:

"Concerning Water." *Freeman* (March 1956): 61–64.

Review of *Cross-Currents*, by Arnold Forster and Benjamin Epstein. *Faith and Freedom* (May 1956): 27; under the pseudonym Aubrey Herbert.

"The Coming Economic Crisis." *National Review* (August 11, 1956): 9–11.

"Government in Business." *Freeman* (September 1956): 39–41. Reprinted in *Essays on Liberty IV*, Irvington-on-Hudson, N.Y.: Foundation for Economic Education, 1958, pp. 183–87.

Review of *The Free Man's Library*, by Henry Hazlitt. *Faith and Freedom* (September 1956): 30–31; under pseudonym Jonathan Randolph. "In Defense of Nasser." Correspondence to *National Review* (September 8, 1956): 22.

"'Yes' and 'No' Plan." Correspondence to *National Review* (October 20, 1956): 16.

Review of *The Anti-Capitalistic Mentality*, by Ludwig von Mises. "Why Anti-Capitalism?" *National Review* (November 10, 1956): 21.

"The Single Tax: Its Economic and Moral Principles." Irvington-on-Hudson, N.Y.: Foundation for Economic Education (November 10, 1956): 1–22. Reprinted as "The Single Tax: Economic and Moral Implications," in 1957 with minor changes.

Review of *Individual Freedom and Governmental Restraints*, by Walter Gellhorn. "Liberal 'Mea Culpa'." *National Review* (December 15, 1956): 20–21.

1957

SCHOLARLY ARTICLES & CHAPTERS IN BOOKS:

"In Defense of 'Extreme Apriorism'." *Southern Economic Journal* 3, no. 23 (January 1957): 314–20. Reprinted in *Austrian Economics*, vol. 1, by Stephen Littlechild. Brookfield, Vt.: Edward Elgar, 1990, pp. 445–51. Translated in French as "L'apriorisme extrême" by François Guillaumat in *Economistes et charlatans*. Paris: Les Belles Lettres, 1991, pp. 83–96. Reprinted in *The Logic of Action One: Method, Money, and the Austrian School*. Cheltenham, U.K.: Edward Elgar, 1997, pp. 100–10. Reprinted and expanded as *Economic Controversies*. Auburn, Ala.: Ludwig von Mises Institute, 2007.

"Huntington on Conservatism: A Comment." *American Political Science Review* 51 (September 1957): 784–87.

OTHER:

Review of *Why Wages Rise*, by F.A. Harper. *National Review* (March 16, 1957): 266.

"Withering From Within." Correspondence to *National Review* (April 20, 1957): 386.

Review of *Economic Institutions and Human Welfare*, by John Maurice Clark. *National Review* (May 11, 1957): 456.

Review of *The Politics of Industry*, by Walton H. Hamilton. *National Review* (June 1, 1957): 529.

"A Reply to Georgist Criticisms." Irvington-on-Hudson, N.Y.: Foundation for Economic Education (July 1957): 1–3. Reprinted in *The Logic of Action Two: Applications and Criticism from the Austrian School*. Cheltenham, U.K.: Edward Elgar, 1997, pp. 306–10. Reprinted and expanded as *Economic Controversies*. Auburn, Ala.: Ludwig von Mises Institute, 2007.

Review of *Citadel, Market and Altar*, by Spencer Heath. *National Review* (September 7, 1957): 214.

Review of *The Labor Policy of a Free Society*, by S. Petrol. *National Review* (September 7, 1957): 214.

Review of *Wage Incentives as a Managerial Tool*, by William B. Wolf. *National Review* (August 3, 1957): 141.

Review of *The King Ranch*, by Tom Lea. *National Review* (October 26, 1957): 382.

Review of *Racial Discrimination and Private Education*, by Arthur S. Miller. *National Review* (December 14, 1957): 548.

"Atlas Shrugged." Communication to *Commonweal* (December 20, 1957): 312–13.

"Good Guys and Bad Guys." *National Review* (December 21, 1957): 569. Reprinted in *Invictus* (February 15, 1970): 6–8.

1958

SCHOLARLY ARTICLES & CHAPTERS IN BOOKS:

"A Note on Burke's *Vindication of Natural Society*." *Journal of the History of Ideas* (January 1958).

OTHER:

Review of *The Grim Truth About Life Insurance*, by Ralph Hendershot. *National Review* (January 18, 1958): 69.

Correspondence to *Modern Age* (Spring, 1958): 220. Re: Herbert Spencer.

Review of *Economic Analysis and Policy in Underdeveloped Countries*, by Peter J. Bauer and *The Economics of Underdeveloped Countries*, by Basil S. Yamey. "Sense on Backward Countries." *National Review* (March 1, 1958): 210–11.

Review of *Lectures On Economic Principles*, by Dennis H. Robertson. *National Review* (April 5, 1958): 332.

"In a Glorious—And Radical—Tradition." *National Review* (June 21, 1958): 14–15.

Review of *Citadel, Market and Altar*, by Spencer Heath. *Freeman* (July 1958): 63–64.

"Present Day Court Historians." *National Review* (September 13, 1958): 186–87.

Review of *Labor Unions and Public Policy*, by Edward H. Chamberlain, Philip D. Bradley, Gerald D. Reilly, and Roscoe Pound. *National Review* (October 25, 1958).

Review of *Foreign Aid Reexamined*, by Helmut Schoeck and James Wiggins, eds. "A Hard Look At Foreign Aid." *National Review* (November 8, 1958): 313–14.

Review of *An Economic Theory of Democracy*, by Anthony Downs. *National Review* (December 28, 1958): 598.

1959

Review of *The Failure of the New Economics*, by Henry Hazlitt. "Challenge to Keynes." *National Review* (August 15, 1959): 279–80.

"Human Rights Are Property Rights." *Freeman* (April 1959): 23–26. Reprinted in *Essays on Liberty* VI. Irvington-on-Hudson, N.Y.: Foundation for Economic Education, 1959, pp. 315–19. Reprinted in Orval V. Watts, ed., *Free Markets or Famine*. Midland, Mich.: Pendell, 1967, pp. 159–62.

"Lewis Strauss and the Constitution." Correspondence to *National Review* (July 18, 1959): 221–22.

"The Bogey of Administered Prices." *Freeman* (September 1959): 39–41.

Review of *Business Cycles and Their Causes* by Welsey Clair Mitchell and *American Business Cycles, 1865–1897*, by Rendigs Fels. *Freeman* (December 1959): 52–54.

Review of *The New Inflation*, by Willard C. Thorp and Rich E. Quandt. *National Review* (December 19, 1959): 561.

1960

SCHOLARLY ARTICLES & CHAPTERS IN BOOKS:

"The Mantle of Science." Helmut Schoeck and James Wiggins, eds., *Scientism and Values*. Princeton, N.J.: D. Van Nostrand, 1960, pp. 159–80. Reprinted in *Individualism and the Philosophy of the Social Sciences*. San Francisco: Cato Institute, Cato Paper, no. 4, 1979, pp. 1–27. Translated in French as "Les oripeaux de la science" by François Guillaumat in *Economistes et charlatans*. Paris: Les Belles Lettres, 1991, pp. 2–38. Reprinted in *The Logic of Action One: Method, Money, and the Austrian School*. Cheltenham, U.K.: Edward Elgar Publishing, 1997, pp. 3–23. Reprinted and expanded as *Economic Controversies*. Auburn, Ala.: Ludwig von Mises Institute, 2007.

"The Politics of Political Economists: Comment." *Quarterly Journal of Economics* (February 1960): 659–65. Reprinted in *The Logic of Action Two: Applications and Criticism from the Austrian School*. Cheltenham, U.K.: Edward Elgar, 1997, pp. 217–25. Reprinted and expanded as *Economic Controversies*. Auburn, Ala.: Ludwig von Mises Institute, 2007.

OTHER:

Review of *A Proper Monetary and Banking System for the United States*, by James Washington Bell and Walter Earl Spahr, eds. *National Review* (July 2, 1960): 436.

"Mr. Rothbard Replies." Correspondence to *National Review* (August 13, 1960): 94.

"Confused Comrades." Correspondence to *National Review* (October 8, 1960): 219.

Review of *The Critics of Keynesian Economics*, by Henry Hazlitt, ed., "One-Two Punch," *National Review* (December 3, 1960): 350–51.

1961

SCHOLARLY ARTICLES & CHAPTERS IN BOOKS:

"Conservatism and Freedom: A Libertarian Comment." *Modern Age* (Spring, 1961): 217–20.

Review of *The Economic Point of View*, by Israel M. Kirzner. "Economics as a Moral Science," *Modern Age* (Spring, 1961): 203–04.

"The Fallacy of the 'Public Sector'." *New Individualist Review* (Summer, 1961): 3–7. Translated in Spanish as "La Fallacia Del Sector Publico." *Orientacion Economical* (Caracas: April 1962). Reprinted in *Temas Contemporaneous* (Mexico City: September 15, 1962). Reprinted as "Cato Essay #1" (San Francisco: Cato Institute, 1978). Translated into Norwegian by Runar Eraker as "Mytem Om Den Offentlige Sektor." *Ideer Om Frihet* 1, no. 4 (December 1980): 11–13. Reprinted in *The Logic of Action Two: Applications and Criticism from the Austrian School*. Cheltenham, U.K.: Edward Elgar, 1997, pp. 171–79. Reprinted and expanded as *Economic Controversies*. Auburn, Ala.: Ludwig von Mises Institute, 2007.

OTHER:

Review of *Turner and Beard*, by Lee Benson. *National Review* (January 14, 1961): 26.

Review of *This Bread Is Mine*, by Robert LeFevre. *National Review* (March 25, 1961): 195.

"Statistics: Achilles' Heel of Government." *Freeman* (June 1961): 40–44. Reprinted in *Essays On Liberty VIII*. Irvington-on-Hudson, N.Y.: Foundation for Economic Education, 1961, pp. 255–61. Reprinted as "Cliche #57, Fact-Finding Is a Proper Function of Government" in *Cliches of Socialism*. Irvington-on-Hudson, N.Y.: Foundation for Economic Education, 1962. Reprinted in *The Logic of Action Two: Applications and Criticism from the Austrian School*. Cheltenham, U.K.: Edward Elgar, 1997, pp. 180–184. Reprinted and expanded as *Economic Controversies*. Auburn, Ala.: Ludwig von Mises Institute, 2007.

Review of *An Inflation Primer*, by Melchior Palyi. *National Review* (June 17, 1961): 394.

"What Is the Proper Way To Study Man?" Reviews of *Epistemological Problems of Economics*, by Ludwig von Mises; *Essays in European Economic Thought* edited by Louise Sommer; *Probability, Statistics and Truth*, by Richard V. Mises. New York: The National Book Foundation (September 15, 1961). Reprinted in *The Logic of Action One: Method, Money, and the Austrian School*. Cheltenham, U.K.: Edward Elgar, 1997, pp. 24–27. Reprinted and expanded as *Economic Controversies*. Auburn, Ala.: Ludwig von Mises Institute, 2007.

1962

BOOKS:

Man, Economy, and State: A Treatise on Economic Principles. 2 vols. Princeton, N.J.: D. Van Nostrand, 1962. Reissue Los Angeles: Nash Publishing, 1970; New York: New York University Press, 1979; Auburn University, Ala.: Ludwig von Mises Institute, 1993 and 2001. Chap. 10 was translated into book form as "Monopolio y Competencia." Buenos Aires: Centro de Estudios Sobre la Libertad, 1965. Chap. 1, app. B was reprinted in *The Logic of Action Two: Applications and Criticism from the Austrian School*. Cheltenham, U.K.: Edward Elgar, 1997, pp. 241–44. The Appendix B of the Conclusion entitled "Collective Goods" and "External Benefits": Two Arguments for Government Activity" was translated into French by François Guillaumat in *Economistes and charlatans*. Paris: Les Belles Lettres, 1991, pp. 164–77. Combined with *Power and Market* for the first time to become *Man, Economy, and State with Power and Market*, Scholar's edition (Auburn, Ala.: Ludwig von Mises Institute, 2004). Translated into Spanish in 2004; Polish and Korean in 2005.

Money, Free and Unfree. Privately circulated manuscript, c. 1962. Published as *Moneda, Libre, y Controlada*. Buenos Aires: Centro de Estu Dios Sobre la Libertad, 1962. Published as *What Has Government Done to Our Money?* Colorado Springs, Colo.:

Pine Tree Press, 1963. Reprinted in the *Washington and Lee Commerce Review* 1, no. 1 (Winter, 1973), pp. 3–51. Reprinted 4th edition, Auburn, Ala.: Ludwig von Mises Institute, 1990. Expanded edition includes *The Case for a 100 Percent Gold Dollar*. Auburn, Ala.: Ludwig von Mises Institute, 2005.

The Panic of 1819: Reactions and Policies. New York: Columbia University Press, 1962. Columbia University Studies in the Social Sciences: no. 605. Reprinted Auburn, Ala.: Ludwig von Mises Institute, 2007.

SCHOLARLY ARTICLES & CHAPTERS IN BOOKS:

"The Case For a 100 Percent Gold Dollar." Leland Yeager, ed., *In Search of a Monetary Constitution*. Cambridge, Mass: Harvard University Press, 1962, pp. 94–136. Reprinted as *The Case For a 100 Percent Gold Dollar*. Washington, D.C.: Libertarian Review Press, 1974; Auburn, Ala.: Ludwig von Mises Institute, 2001. Included in *What Has Government Done to Our Money?* Auburn, Ala.: Ludwig von Mises Institute, 2005.

Review of *Freedom and the Law*, by B. Leoni. "On Freedom and the Law." *New Individualist Review* (Winter, 1962): 37–40.

"Epistemological Problems of Economics: Comment." *Southern Economic Journal* 28, no. 4 (April 1962): 385–87.

"H.L. Mencken: The Joyous Libertarian." *New Individualist Review* (Summer, 1962: 15–27. Reprinted in *Reason* (December 1980).

OTHER:

"Why, You'd Take Us Back To the Horse and Buggy." Cliche, no. 7 in *Cliches of Socialism*. Irvington-on-Hudson, N.Y.: Foundation for Economic Education, 1962, pp. 20–22. Reprinted in *The Law and Cliches of Socialism*. Whittier, Calif.: Constructive Action, 1964, pp. 102–04.

1963

BOOKS:

America's Great Depression. Princeton, N.J.: D. Van Nostrand, 1963. Reissued, Los Angeles: Nash Publishing, 1972 with introduction to the 2nd edition. Revised edition, New York: New York University Press, 1975. New York: Richardson and Snyder, 1983. Introduction to the 5th edition by Paul Johnson, Auburn, Ala.: Ludwig von Mises Institute, 2000. Translated into Chinese and Italian in 2003; Polish in 2006. Presented as an audio book by Blackstone Audiobooks in 2005.

What Has Government Done to Our Money? Colorado Springs, Colo.: Pine Tree Press, 1963. Reprinted in the Washington and Lee *Commerce Review* 1, no. 1 (Winter, 1973): 3–51. Reprinted 4th edition. Auburn, Ala.: Ludwig von Mises Institute, 1990. Originally circulated unpublished under the title *Money, Free and Unfree*, c. 1962. Published as *Moneda, Libre, y Controlada*. Buenos Aires: Centro de Estu Dios Sobre la Libertad, 1962. Expanded 4th edition includes *The Case for a 100 Percent Gold Dollar*. Auburn, Ala.: Ludwig von Mises Institute, 2005. Translated into Polish in 2002; into Spanish 2003; Chinese in 2004; Romanian in 2005; Turkish in 2006.

SCHOLARLY ARTICLES & CHAPTERS IN BOOKS:

"Money, the State and Modern Mercantilism." *Modern Age* (Summer, 1963): 279–89. Reprinted in Helmut Schoeck and James Wiggins, eds. *Central Planning and Neo-Mercantilism*. Princeton, N.J.: D. Van Nostrand, 1964, pp. 138–54. Reprinted in *The Logic of Action One: Method, Money, and the Austrian School*. Cheltenham, U.K.: Edward Elgar, 1997, pp. 321–36. Reprinted and expanded as *Economic Controversies*. Auburn, Ala.: Ludwig von Mises Institute, 2007.

"The Negro Revolution." *New Individualist Review* (Summer, 1963): 29–37.

"The Frankfort Resolutions and the Panic of 1819." *The Register of the Kentucky Historical Society* (July 1963).

"The Logic and Semantics of Government." *Pacific Philosophy Forum* (December 1963).

OTHER:

"War, Peace, and the State." *The Standard* (April 1963): 2–5, 15–16.

"Restrictionist Pricing of Labor." *Freeman* (May 1963): 11–16. Reprinted in *The Logic of Action Two: Applications and Criticism from the Austrian School*. Cheltenham, U.K.: Edward Elgar, 1997, pp. 36–42. Reprinted and expanded as *Economic Controversies*. Auburn, Ala.: Ludwig von Mises Institute, 2007.

"Mercantilism: A Lesson For Our Times?" *Freeman* (November 1963): 16–27. Reprinted in *Essays On Liberty XI*. Irvington-on-Hudson, N.Y.: Foundation for Economic Education, pp. 182–200. Translated as "El Mercantilismo: Una Leccion De Nuestros Tiempos?" *Ideas Sobre La Libertad* (November 1970). Reprinted in *The Logic of Action Two: Applications and Criticism from the Austrian School*. Cheltenham, U.K.: Edward Elgar, 1997, pp. 43–55. Reprinted and expanded as *Economic Controversies*. Auburn, Ala.: Ludwig von Mises Institute, 2007.

1964

"Transformation of the American Right." *Continuum* (Summer, 1964): 220–31.

"Repartee—To Miss Leach." Correspondence to *Liberal Innovator* (August 1964): 27.

1965

SCHOLARLY ARTICLES & CHAPTERS IN BOOKS:

"The Anatomy of the State." *Rampart Journal* (Summer, 1965): 1–24. Reprinted in Tibor R. Machan, ed., *The Libertarian Alternative*. Chicago: Nelson-Hall, 1974, pp. 69–93.

OTHER:

Review of *What is Conservatism*, by Frank S. Meyer, ed., "A Good Question?" *Continuum* (Winter, 1965): 714–17.

"Justice and Property Rights." *Innovator* (January 1965): 10–11.

"The General Line," "Left and Right: The Prospects for Liberty." *Left and Right* 1, no. 1 (Spring, 1965).

"Left and Right: The Prospects for Liberty" was reprinted in Tibor R. Machan, ed., *The Libertarian Alternative*. Chicago: Nelson-Hall, 1974, pp. 525–49; it was also reprinted in *Left and Right, Selected Essays 1954–1965*. New York: Arno Press, 1972.

"The Spooner-Tucker Doctrine, From the Point of View of an Economist." *A Way Out* (May–July 1965).

"Get Out of Vietnam!" *Innovator* (July 1965).

"Fortune and American 'Idealism'," "Discovering the Ninth Amendment," "Liberty and the New Left." *Left and Right* 1, no. 2 (Autumn, 1965): 35–67.

1966

SCHOLARLY ARTICLES & CHAPTERS IN BOOKS:

"Bertrand de Jouvenel e i diritti di proprieta." *Biblioteca Della Liberta* (Torino, Italy; May-June 1966).

"Herbert Clark Hoover: A Reconsideration." *New Individualist Review* (Winter, 1966): 3–12.

Review of *The Poverty of Abundance: Hoover, the Nation, the Depression*, by Albert U. Romasco. "The Hoover Myth," *Studies on the Left* (July-August 1966): 70–84. Reprinted in James Weinstein and David Eakins, eds., *For a New America: Essays in History and Politics From Studies on the Left, 1959–1967*. New York: Random House, 1970, pp. 162–79.

OTHER:

"Old Right/New Left," "New Right: *National Review*'s Anniversary," "From Georgia With Love: The Case of Julian Bond," "The Mitchell Case." *Left and Right* 2, no. 1 (Winter, 1966).

"On the Importance of Revisionism For Our Time." *Rampart Journal* (Spring, 1966): 3–7.

"The Irish Revolution," "The Power of the President," "Labor Unionism, Two Views," "Our Fifth Anniversary." *Left and Right* 2, no. 2 (Spring, 1966). "Robert Schuchman—As His Friends Remember Him." *New Guard* (April 1966).

"Albert Jay Nock, Radical." *Fragments* (April-June 1966): 8.

"Why Be Libertarian?," "The Cry for Power: Black, White, and 'Polish'," "The Martyrdom of Earl Francis," "Pearl Harbor: Twenty-Fifth Anniversary." *Left and Right* 2, no. 3 (Autumn, 1966).

"The First Liberty Library." *Freeman* (October 1966): 56–59.

1967

SCHOLARLY ARTICLES & CHAPTERS IN BOOKS:

"The Great Society: A Libertarian Critique." Marvin Gettlemen and David Mermelstein, eds., *The Great Society Reader: The Failure of American Liberalism*. New York: Random House, 1967, pp. 502–11. Reprinted in 2nd edition, 1971. Reprinted in Richard Romano and Melvin Leiman, eds., *Views on Capitalism*. Beverly Hills, Calif.: Glencoe Press, 1970, pp. 86–94. Reprinted in Robert Carson, Jerry Ingles, and Douglas McLaud, eds., *Government in the American Economy*. Lexington, Mass.: D.C. Heath, 1973, pp. 88–94.

"Economic Thought: Comment." David T. Gilchrist, ed., *The Growth of the Seaport Cities, 1790–1825*. Charlottesville: University Press of Virginia, 1967, pp. 178–84.

OTHER:

Review of *The Moulding of Communists: The Training of the Communist Cadre*, by Frank Meyer. c. 1967.

"Frank Chodorov: RIP," "SDS: The New Turn," "Is There a Nazi Threat?" "Liberalism and the CIA." *Left and Right* 3, no. 1 (Winter, 1967).

"Frank Chodorov: Individualist." *Fragments* (January-March 1967): 13. Reprinted in *Fragments* (October-December 1980): 11.

"Frank Meyer on the Communist Bogey Man." *Left and Right* 3, no. 2 (Spring-Summer, 1967).

"Education in California." *Colorado Springs Gazette Telegraph* (Pine Tree Column), 9 May 1967. Reprinted in the *Orange County Register*, 13 May 1967.

"Reaching for the Zoning Club." *Colorado Springs Gazette Telegraph* (Pine Tree Column), 14 May 1967.

"Abolish Slavery–Part I." *Colorado Springs Gazette Telegraph* (Pine Tree Column), 23 May 1967. Reprinted in the *Orange County Register*, 17 June 1967.

"Abolish Slavery–Part II." *Colorado Springs Gazette Telegraph* (Pine Tree Column), 24 May 1967. Reprinted in the *Orange County Register*, 19 June 1967.

"Abolish Slavery–Part III." *Colorado Springs Gazette Telegraph* (Pine Tree Column), 8 June 1967. Reprinted in the *Orange County Register*, 22 June 1967.

"The Middle East Crisis." *Colorado Springs Gazette Telegraph* (Pine Tree Column), 16 June 1967. Reprinted as "The Crisis In The Middle East" in the *Orange County Register*, 18 June 1967.

"The Stirnerite Stand on Aggression and Invasion." Letter to *Minus One* (July 1967): 3–4.

"Abolish Slavery–Part IV." *Colorado Springs Gazette Telegraph* (Pine Tree Column), 2 July 1967.

"We're in a Recession." *Colorado Springs Gazette Telegraph* (Pine Tree Column), 6 July 1967. Reprinted in the *Orange County Register*, 12 July 1967.

"Abolish Slavery!" *Colorado Springs Gazette Telegraph* (Pine Tree Column), 13 July 1967. Reprinted as "Abolish Slavery: Compulsory Jury Duty Also Is Draft" in the *Orange County Register*, 3 August 1967.

"Abolish Slavery–Part V." *Colorado Springs Gazette Telegraph* (Pine Tree Column), 18 July 1967.

"'Little' Israel." *Colorado Springs Gazette Telegraph* (Pine Tree Column), 22 July 1967. Reprinted as "'Little' Israel's Blitzkrieg" in the *Orange County Register*, 24 July 1967.

"'Rebellion' at Newark." *Colorado Springs Gazette Telegraph* (Pine Tree Column), 29 July 1967.

"Ernesto Che Guevara, RIP," "The Black Revolution," "On Desecrating the Flag," "War Guilt in the Middle East." *Left and Right* 3, no. 3 (Autumn, 1967).

"Should There Be Another Tax Hike?–Part I." *Colorado Springs Gazette Telegraph* (Pine Tree Column), 19 September 1967.

"Should There Be Another Tax Hike?–Part II." *Colorado Springs Gazette Telegraph* (Pine Tree Column), 27 September 1967.

"A Way Out." Letter to S.E. Parker, October 1967, pp. 12–13.

"The Principle of Secession Defended." *Colorado Springs Gazette Telegraph* (Pine Tree Column), 3 October 1967.

"Which Statement Was More Irrational?" *Orange County Register*, 5 October 1967.

"Abolish Slavery!" *Colorado Springs Gazette Telegraph* (Pine Tree Column), 10 October 1967. Reprinted in the *Orange County Register*, 15 October 1967.

"Businessmen for Peace." *Colorado Springs Gazette Telegraph* (Pine Tree Column), 20 October 1967.

"Gun Laws." *Colorado Springs Gazette Telegraph* (Pine Tree Column), 25 October 1967. Reprinted in the *Orange County Register*, 14 November 1967.

"'Incitement' to Riot." *Colorado Springs Gazette Telegraph* (Pine Tree Column), 29 October 1967.

"LBJ–After Four Years." *Colorado Springs Gazette Telegraph* (Pine Tree Column), 8 November 1967. Reprinted as "All That Glitters" in the *Orange County Register*, 11 November 1967.

"A New Constitution?" *Colorado Springs Gazette Telegraph* (Pine Tree Column), 18 November 1967. Reprinted as "Who Wants A New Constitution?" in the *Orange County Register*, 18 November 1967.

"Optimism After 1967 Elections." *Orange County Register*, 25 November 1967. Reprinted as "The Elections" in *Colorado Springs Gazette Telegraph* (Pine Tree Column), 2 December 1967.

"Why Do They all Hate France's De Gaulle?" *Colorado Springs Gazette Telegraph* (Pine Tree Column), 3 December 1967. Reprinted in the *Orange County Register*, 4 December 1967.

"The Cyprus Question." *Colorado Springs Gazette Telegraph* (Pine Tree Column), 14 December 1967.

"How to Get Out of Vietnam." *Colorado Springs Gazette Telegraph* (Pine Tree Column), 15 December 1967.

"Partition Seen As Solution." *Orange County Register*, 17 December 1967.

"The Case of John Milton Ratliff." *Colorado Springs Gazette Telegraph* (Pine Tree Column), 24 December 1967.

1968

SCHOLARLY ARTICLES & CHAPTERS IN BOOKS:

"Biography of Ludwig von Mises." *International Encyclopedia of Social Sciences* XVI (1968): 379–82.

"Harry Elmer Barnes As Revisionist of the Cold War." Arthur Goddard, ed., *Harry Elmer Barnes, Learned Crusader: The New History in Action*. Colorado Springs, Colo.: Ralph Myles, 1968, pp. 314–30.

OTHER:

"Jim Garrison, Libertarian." *Colorado Springs Gazette Telegraph* (Pine Tree Column), 7 January 1968.

"Whose Violence?" *Colorado Springs Gazette Telegraph* (Pine Tree Column), 14 January 1968.

"Devaluation Will Come!" *Orange County Register*, 20 January 1968. Reprinted as "Devaluation" in *Colorado Springs Gazette Telegraph* (Pine Tree Column), 22 January 1968.

"Exchange Controls." *Colorado Springs Gazette Telegraph* (Pine Tree Column), 28 January 1968.

"The Pueblo Caper." *Colorado Springs Gazette Telegraph* (Pine Tree Column), January 1968.

"Coming American Fascism." *Colorado Springs Gazette Telegraph* (Pine Tree Column), 8 February 1968.

"The State of the War." *Colorado Springs Gazette Telegraph* (Pine Tree Column), 23 February 1968.

"The Garbage Strike." *Colorado Springs Gazette Telegraph* (Pine Tree Column), 3 March 1968.

"The Vietnam Crisis." *Colorado Springs Gazette Telegraph* (Pine Tree Column), 10 March 1968.

"The Escalation of Lyndon Johnson." *Colorado Springs Gazette Telegraph* (Pine Tree Column), 30 March 1968.

"The Amateur." *Colorado Springs Gazette Telegraph* (Pine Tree Column), 31 March 1968.

"What Does the Viet Cong Want?" *Colorado Springs Gazette Telegraph* (Pine Tree Column), 12 April 1968.

"April Fool Week." *Colorado Springs Gazette Telegraph* (Pine Tree Column), 23 April 1968.

"Martin Luther King." *Colorado Springs Gazette Telegraph* (Pine Tree Column), 29 April 1968.

"All the Withdrawals." *Colorado Springs Gazette Telegraph* (Pine Tree Column), 1 May 1968.

"The Peace Negotiations." *Colorado Springs Gazette Telegraph* (Pine Tree Column), 9 May 1968.

"Shooting Looters." *Colorado Springs Gazette Telegraph* (Pine Tree Column), 25 May 1968.

Review of *Economic Thought in the Ante-Bellum South*, by Melvin Leiman and Jacob N. Cardozo. *Political Science Quarterly* (June 1968): 299–300.

"The Revolutionary Mood." *Colorado Springs Gazette Telegraph* (Pine Tree Column), 8 June 1968.

"Confessions of a Right-Wing Liberal." *Ramparts* (June 15, 1968): 48–52. Reprinted in *Schism* (Summer, 1969). Reprinted in Henry J. Silverman, ed., *American Radical Thought: The Libertarian Tradition*. Lexington, Mass.: D.C. Heath, 1970, pp. 291–99.

"Assassinations–Left and Right." *Colorado Springs Gazette Telegraph* (Pine Tree Column), 21 June 1968.

"French Revolution–1968." *Colorado Springs Gazette Telegraph* (Pine Tree Column), c. June 1968.

"Draft Boards." *Colorado Springs Gazette Telegraph* (Pine Tree Column), 3 July 1968.

"The Student Revolution." *Colorado Springs Gazette Telegraph* (Pine Tree Column), 16 July 1968.

"Humphrey or Nixon: Is There Any Difference?" *Colorado Springs Gazette Telegraph* (Pine Tree Column), 8 August 1968.

"About Burnham." Letter to *National Review*, 13 August 1968, pp. 7–8. Re: Right-wing conservatism and libertarianism.

1969

BOOKS:

Economic Depressions: Causes and Cures. Lansing, Mich.: Constitutional Alliance, 1969. Constitutes part of the National Issues Series of Politics 4, no. 8. Reprinted in Richard Ebeling, ed., *The Austrian Theory of the Trade Cycle and Other Essays*, Occasional Paper Series #8. New York: Center for Libertarian Studies, 1978, pp. 21–34. Washington, D.C.: Ludwig von Mises Institute, 1983.

OTHER:

"Libertarian Strategy: Part I." *Libertarian Connection*, 10 February 1969.

"Why 'The Libertarian'?" "The Nixon Administration: Creeping Cornuelism," "State of Palastine Launched," "Private Enterprise at Work," "Sitting on Sidewalk Outlawed," "Recommended Reading." *The Libertarian Forum* Preview Issue (March 1, 1969).

"The Scientific Imperial Counsellor: 'To Restore Faith in Government'," "'Dear Ted': Prelude to Repression?" "Recommended Reading." *The Libertarian Forum* 1, no. 1 (April 1, 1969).

"Tax Day," "Tax Revolt in Wisconsin," "Recommended Reading." *The Libertarian Forum* 1, no. 2 (April 15, 1969).

"The Student Revolution." *The Libertarian Forum* 1, no. 3 (May 1, 1969).

"Mailer for Mayor," "The Panthers and Black Liberation," "Recommended Reading." *The Libertarian Forum* 1, no. 4 (May 15, 1969).

"Libertarian Strategy: Part II." *Libertarian Connection*, 17 May 1969.

"Libertarian Strategy: Part III." *Libertarian Connection*, 17 May 1969.

"The Movement Grows," "Recommended Reading." *The Libertarian Forum* 1, no. 5 (June 1, 1969).

"Massacre at People's Park," "Change of Name," "Confiscation and the Homestead Principle," "Recommended Reading." *The Libertarian Forum* 1, no. 6 (June 15, 1969).

"The Meaning of Revolution," "Defense Funds," "Recommended Reading." *The Libertarian Forum* 1, no. 7 (July 1, 1969).

"Nixon's Decisions," "Recommended Reading." *The Libertarian Forum* 1, no. 8 (July 15, 1969).

"Revolt in Minnesota," "Nelson's Waterloo," "The New Deal and Fascism," "Recommended Reading." *The Libertarian Forum* 1, no. 9 (August 1, 1969).

"Libertarian Strategy: Part IV." *Libertarian Connection*, 9 August 1969.

"Libertarian Strategy: Part V." *Libertarian Connection*, 9 August 1969.

"Listen, YAF." *The Libertarian Forum* 1, no. 10 (1969).

"The Guaranteed Annual Income." *Rational Individualist* (September 1969): 6–9.

"National Liberation." *The Libertarian Forum* 1, no. 11 (August 15, 1969).

"YAF Power Play," "Note on Libertarians," "Recommended Reading." *The Libertarian Forum* 1, no. 12 (September 15, 1969).

"Anarcho-Rightism," "The New Boston Tea Party," "*National Review* Rides Again," "Abolition: An Acid Test," "Recommended Reading." *The Libertarian Forum* 1, no. 13 (October 1969).

"We Make the Media." *The Libertarian Forum* 1, no. 14 (October 15, 1969).

"The Conference," "Recommended Reading." *The Libertarian Forum* 1, no. 15 (November 1, 1969).

"Ultra-Leftism," "Attention, Libertarians," "A YAF Conversion," "Recommended Reading." *The Libertarian Forum* 1, no. 16 (November 15, 1969).

Review of *The Corporate Ideal in the Liberal State, 1900–1918*, by James Weinstein. *Ramparts* (December 1969): 38–40.

"The Anti-War Movement," "Recommended Reading." *The Libertarian Forum* 1, no. 17 (December 1, 1969).

"Notes on Repression." *The Libertarian Forum* 1, no. 18 (December 15, 1969).

1970

BOOKS:

Power and Market: Government and the Economy. Menlo Park, Calif.: Institute for Humane Studies, 1970. Kansas City: Sheed Andrews and McMeel, 1977. Auburn, Ala.: Ludwig von Mises Institute, 2006. Combined with *Man, Economy, and State* to become *Man, Economy, and State with Power and Market.* Auburn, Ala.: Ludwig von Mises Institute, 2004. Translated into Polish in 2005; Croatian in 2005.

SCHOLARLY ARTICLES & CHAPTERS IN BOOKS:

"The Hoover Myth," in James Weinstein and David Eakins, eds., *For a New America: Essays in History and Politics From Studies on the Left, 1959–1967.* New York: Random House, 1970, pp. 162–179. Originally a review of *The Poverty of Abundance,* by Arthur U. Romasco that appeared in *Studies on the Left* (July-August 1966): 70–84.

OTHER:

"Individualist Anarchism in the United States: The Origins." *Libertarian Analysis* (Winter, 1970): 14–28.

"Anarcho-Communism." *The Libertarian Forum* 2, no. 1 (January 1, 1970).

"What's Your Excuse Now?" "Against Taxation," "USIA Network." *The Libertarian Forum* 2, no. 2 (January 15, 1970).

"The Great Ecology Issue: Conservation in *The Free Market* (February 1970): 1–6.

"Biafra, RIP." *The Libertarian Forum* 2, no. 3 (February 1, 1970).

"The Task Ahead," "Meet Libertarians," "Recommended Reading." *The Libertarian Forum* 2, no. 4 (February 15, 1970).

"Who Needs Military Spending?" *Dollars and Sense* (March 1971): 8.

"Free Bill Kunstler!" "Renew! Subscribe!" "Doctors and Drugs," "Postal Note," "Recommended Reading." *The Libertarian Forum* 2, no. 5 (March 1, 1970).

"The Great Defense Spending Issue." *Individualist* (March-April 1970): 5–6.

"The New Left, RIP," "For a New America." *The Libertarian Forum* 2, no. 6 (March 15, 1970).

"The Mad Bombers," "The Knudson Revolt," "Articles Welcome," "Recommended Reading." *The Libertarian Forum* 2, no. 7 (April 1, 1970).

"The Individualist," "The Tuccille Book," "Recommended Reading." *The Libertarian Forum* 2, no. 8 (April 15, 1970).

"The Great Women's Liberation Issue: Setting It Straight." *Individualist* (May 1970): 1–7.

"Farewell to the Left," "Recommended Reading." *The Libertarian Forum* 2, no. 9 (May 1, 1970).

"The Great Inflationary Recession Issue: 'Nixonomics' Explained." *Individualist* (June 1970): 1–5.

"The New Movement: Peace Politics," "The Judges," "Movers, Write!" *The Libertarian Forum* 2, no. 11 (June 1, 1970).

"The Nixon Mess," "Abortion Repeal," "From the 'Old Curmudgeon'," "Recommended Reading." *The Libertarian Forum* 2, no. 12 (June 15, 1970).

"On Civil Obedience," "From the 'Old Curmudgeon'," "Recommended Reading." *The Libertarian Forum* 2, nos. 13–14 (July 1970).

"Hatfield for President?" *The Libertarian Forum* 2, nos. 15–16 (August 1970).

Review of *Corporations and the Cold War*, by David Horowitz, ed. *Ramparts* (September 1970): 50–52.

"The Socialist Scholars Caper," "More on Money," "Recommended Reading." *The Libertarian Forum* 2, no. 17 (September 1, 1970).

"When Revolution?" "The Case for Elites," "From the 'Old Curmudgeon'," "Gems of Statism." *The Libertarian Forum* 2, no. 19 (October 1, 1970).

"Polarization," "Recommended Reading." *The Libertarian Forum* 2, no. 20 (October 15, 1970).

Review of *Radical Libertarianism*, by Jerome Tuccille. *Choice* (November 1970): 1300. (Unsigned)

"White Terror in Quebec," "Gems of Statism," "Recommended Reading." *The Libertarian Forum* 2, no. 21 (November 1, 1970).

"The Elections," "Retreat from Freedom," "Stirrings, Right and Left." *The Libertarian Forum* 2, nos. 22–23 (November 15–December 1, 1970).

Review of *Goliath*, by David Harris. *Choice* (December 1970): 1408. (Unsigned)

"Death of the Left," "Hawaii–Growth and Repression," "Anarchism–A New Convert," "Recommended Reading." *The Libertarian Forum* 2, no. 24 (December 15, 1970).

1971

SCHOLARLY ARTICLES & CHAPTERS IN BOOKS:

"Lange, Mises and Praxeology: The Retreat from Marxism." *Toward Liberty* 2 (Menlo Park, Calif.: Institute for Humane Studies, 1971), pp. 307–21. Reprinted in *The Logic of Action One: Method, Money, and the Austrian School*. Cheltenham, U.K.: Edward Elgar, 1997, pp. 384–96. Reprinted and expanded as *Economic Controversies*. Auburn, Ala.: Ludwig von Mises Institute, 2007.

"Freedom, Inequality, Primitivism and the Division of Labor." *Modern Age* (Summer, 1971): 226–45. Reprinted in Kenneth S. Templeton, Jr., ed., *The Politicization of Society*. Indianapolis: Liberty Press, 1979, pp. 83–126. Reprinted in *The Logic of Action Two: Applications and Criticism from the Austrian School*. Cheltenham, U.K.: Edward Elgar, 1997, pp. 3–35. Reprinted and expanded as *Economic Controversies*. Auburn, Ala.: Ludwig von Mises Institute, 2007.

"Ludwig von Mises and the Paradigm of Our Age." *Modern Age* (Fall, 1971): 370–79. Reprinted in *The Logic of Action One: Method, Money, and the Austrian School*.

Cheltenham, U.K.: Edward Elgar, 1997, pp. 195–210. Reprinted and expanded as *Economic Controversies*. Auburn, Ala.: Ludwig von Mises Institute, 2007.

OTHER:

"Defusing the Baby Bomb." *Individualist* (January 1971): 1–4.

"Nixonite Socialism," "To Our Readers," "Social Darwinism Reconsidered," "Knee-Jerk Radicalism," "Recommended Reading." *The Libertarian Forum* 3, no. 1 (January 1971).

Review of *Anarchism*, by R. Hoffman, ed., *Choice* (January 1971): 1577. (Unsigned)

"Milton Friedman Unraveled." *Individualist* (February 1971): 3–7.

"Takeoff," "Come One! Come All!" "Correction," "Living Free," "Recommended Reading." *The Libertarian Forum* 3, no. 2 (February 1971).

Review of *In Defense of Anarchism*, by Robert Paul Wolff. *Choice* (March 1971): 143. (Unsigned)

"Takeoff II," "Recommended Reading," "From the 'Old Curmudgeon'." *The Libertarian Forum* 3, no. 3 (March 1971). (Note: The masthead reads "No. 2" in error.)

"Know Your Rights." *Win* (March 1, 1971): 6–10. Reprinted in *Schism* (Summer, 1971).

"Education: Free and Compulsory" (Part I). *Individualist* (April 1971): 2–8.

"The Conning of America," "First Midwest Libertarian Festival," "Libertarian Conference," "Army Intelligence Reads the Forum." *The Libertarian Forum* 3, no. 4 (April 1971).

"Inflation and Taxes." *Dollars and Sense* (May 1971).

"Orwell Lives," "From the 'Old Curmudgeon'," "Contempt for the Usual," "Is Pot Harmless?" "Recommended Reading," "We Beat the SST," "Libertarian Book News," "For Bengal." *The Libertarian Forum* 3, no. 5 (May 1971).

"How to Destatize," "Syndical Syndrome," "Jerome Daly Once More," Recommended Reading," "The Senate and the Draft," "Nixonite Socialism." *The Libertarian Forum* 3, no. 5 (June 1971). (Note: This is the second "Vol. 3, no. 5.")

Review of *Selected Writings*, by P. Kropotkin. *Choice* (June 1971): 610. (Unsigned)

"Dumping Nixon," "Comment," "From the 'Old Curmudgeon'." *The Libertarian Forum* 3, nos. 6–7 (July-August 1971).

"Education: Free and Compulsory" (Part II). *Individualist* (July-August, 1971): 3–16.

"Is This the Death of the Free Market?" *Rocky Mountain News Global*, 22 August 1971.

Review of *The Wisdom of Conservatism*, by Peter Witonski, ed. *Choice* (September 1971): 912. (Unsigned)

"The President's Economic Betrayal." *The New York Times*, 4 September 1971, p. 21. Reprinted as "Wage Price Freeze" in *The Stanford Daily*, date unknown.

"Attica," "Reprint Bonanza," "Recommended Reading." *The Libertarian Forum* 3, no. 9 (October 1971).

"The End of Economic Freedom," "You Read It Here." *The Libertarian Forum* 3, no. 8 (September 1971).

"The End of Economic Freedom" reprinted in the *Individualist* (October 1971): 2–7.

"Laissez Faire Called Fairest System of All." *New York Sunday News*, 17 October 1971.

"Nixon's NAP." *Individualist* (October 1971): 8–11. Reprinted from *The Libertarian Forum* (November 1971).

"Nixon's Nep," "We Fight the Freeze," "Libertarian Wit." *The Libertarian Forum* 3, no. 10 (November 1971).

"The UN and the War," "Mises *Festschrift*," "Recommended Reading," "Libertarian Conference." *The Libertarian Forum* 3, no. 11 (December 1971).

"Why Be Libertarian?" *The Abolitionist* (December 1971): 1–5.

1972

BOOKS:

Education, Free and Compulsory: The Individual's Education. Wichita, Kans.: Center for Independent Education, 1972. Reprinted Auburn Ala.: Ludwig von Mises Institute, 1999.

Left and Right, Selected Essays 1954–1965. New York: Arno Press, 1972.

The Libertarian Forum (1969–1971). Rothbard and Karl Hess, eds. New York: Arno Press, 1972. Reprinted by Ayer, 1972.

SCHOLARLY ARTICLES & CHAPTERS IN BOOKS:

"Capitalism versus Statism." Dorothy B. James, ed., *Outside Looking In: Critiques of American Policies and Institutions, Left and Right*. New York: Harper and Row, 1972, pp. 60–74. Reprinted in *The Logic of Action Two: Applications and Criticism from the Austrian School*. Cheltenham, U.K.: Edward Elgar, 1997, pp. 185–99. Reprinted and expanded as *Economic Controversies*. Auburn, Ala.: Ludwig von Mises Institute, 2007.

"Herbert Hoover and the Myth of Laissez Faire." Ronald Radosh and Rothbard, eds., *A New History of Leviathan*. New York: E.P. Dutton, 1972, pp. 111–45.

"War Collectivism in World War I." Ronald Radosh and Rothbard, eds., *A New History of Leviathan*. New York: E.P. Dutton, 1972, pp. 66–110.

Review of *Roads to Freedom: Essays in Honor of Friedrich A. von Hayek*, by Erich Streissler, Gottfried Habeler, Friedrich A. Lutz, and Fritz Machlup, eds. *Political Science Quarterly* (March 1972): 162–63.

Review of *Economic Means and Social Ends*, by Robert Heilbroner. *The Antitrust Bulletin* (Summer, 1972): 691–700. Reprinted as "Heilbroner's *Economic Means and Social Ends*" in *The Logic of Action Two: Applications and Criticism from the Austrian School*. Cheltenham, U.K.: Edward Elgar, 1997, pp. 260–68. Reprinted and expanded as *Economic Controversies*. Auburn, Ala.: Ludwig von Mises Institute, 2007.

OTHER:

Introduction to *Propaganda for the Next War*, by Sidney Rogerson. New York: Garland Publishing, 1972. (Reprint.)

Preface to *A New History of Leviathan*, by Ronald Radosh and Rothbard, eds. New York: E.P. Dutton, 1972, pp. v–ix.

"Politics '72," "Libertarianism Versus Controls." *The Libertarian Forum* 4, no. 1 (January 1972).

Review of *The Anarchists*, by Roderick Kedward. *Choice* (January 1972): 1510.

"Phase II is Cracking," "The Political Circus," "Of Interest to Libertarians," "For Croatia," "Will the Real (Howard Hughes, . . .) Please Stand Up!" "The Movement Marches On," "Recommended Reading," "From the 'Old Curmudgeon'." *The Libertarian Forum* 4, no. 2 (February 1972).

Interview with Rothbard. *The New Banner* (February 25, 1972). Reprinted in *Schism* (Summer, 1972): 21–27.

"The Party," "The Political Circus," "From the 'Old Curmudgeon'." *The Libertarian Forum* 4, no. 3 (March 1972).

"The Value-Added Tax Is Not the Answer." *Human Events* (March 11, 1972): 197. Appears in the *Congressional Record* (March 14, 1972). Reprinted in *The Stanford Daily* in two parts as "VAT—Dangerous Swindle," 4 May 1972 and 9 May 1972.

"A Bunch of Losers," "Short People, Arise!" *The Libertarian Forum* 4, no. 4 (April 1972).

Review of *It Usually Begins With Ayn Rand*, by Jerome Tuccille. *Choice* (April 1972): 283. (Unsigned)

"Should Libertarians Vote?" *Outlook* (April 1972): 6.

"Nixon's World," "The Party Once More," "From the 'Old Curmudgeon'," "The Shadow Cabinet," "Recommended Reading," "Frank S Meyer, RIP." *The Libertarian Forum* 4, no. 5 (May 1972).

"McGovern???" "The Party Emerges," "Another Lone Nut?" "Arts and Movies." *The Libertarian Forum* 4 Nos. 6–7 (June-July 1972).

"Mao As Free Enterprise, Or, Halbrook in Wonderland." *Outlook* (July-August 1972): 6–7.

Review of *Anarchism Today*, by David Apter and James Joll, eds., *Choice* (July-August 1972): 714. (Unsigned)

Review of *Freedom and the Law*, by Bruno Leoni. *National Review* (July 21, 1972): 803–04.

"Bombing the Dikes," (Testimony before the International War Crimes Tribunal, 1967.) *The Libertarian Forum* 4, nos. 8–9 (August-September 1972).

Review of *Conservative Mind in America*, by Ronald Lora. *Choice* (September 1972): 882. (Unsigned)

"Nix On McGovernment." *Outlook* (October 1972): 8–10, 22.

"November???" "No, No McGovern," "Archy's Last Gasp?" "The Schmitz Ticket," "Unit or Cadre," "Recommended Reading." *The Libertarian Forum* 4, no. 8 (October 1972).

"Beyond the Sixties," "From the 'Old Curmudgeon'," "The Senate Rated," "The Elections," "Whither Democracy?" "Recommended Reading," "Arts and Movies." *The Libertarian Forum* 4, no. 9 (November 1972).

Correspondence to *Forum For Contemporary History*, 17 November 1972. Appears in condensed form in *Intellectual Digest* (January or February 1973) as "The Quota System, in Short, Must Be Repudiated Immediately." Reprinted as "Quotas Must Be Repudiated" in *The Stanford Daily*, 27 April 1973.

Gold & Silver Newsletter. Long Beach, Calif.: Pacific Coast Coin Exchange, 30 November 1972. Reprinted in Louis E. Carabini, ed., *Everything You Need To Know About Gold and Silver*. New Rochelle, N.Y.: Arlington House, 1974.

"Controls Won't Work." *Intellectual Digest* (December 1972): 56–57.

"Kid Lib." *Outlook* (December 1972): 8–10.

Review of *The Literature of Isolationism: A Guide To Non-Interventionist Scholarship 1930–1972*, by Justus Doenecke. *Books for Libertarians* (December 1972).

"The Movement," "Hospers on Crime and the FBI," "From the 'Old Curmudgeon'," "We Make the Electoral College!" "Freedom, Pot, and *National Review*," "Recommended Reading," "The Editor Replies," "Bormann Once More." *The Libertarian Forum* 4, no. 10 (December 1972).

1973

BOOKS:

For A New Liberty: The Libertarian Manifesto. New York: Macmillan, 1973. Revised edition with preface and a new chapter 1, "The Libertarian Heritage." New York: Collier Books, 1978. Excerpt reprinted in *The Libertarian Reader*, by David Boaz, ed. New York: The Free Press, 1997, p. 367. Transalted into Italian in 2003; Spanish in 2004; Greek in 2005.

The Essential von Mises. Lansing, Mich.: Bramble Minibooks, 1973. Reprinted 4th edition in Ludwig von Mises, *Planning for Freedom*. South Holland, Ill.: Libertarian Press, 1980, pp. 234–70. Reprinted Washington, D.C: Ludwig von Mises Institute, 1983. Translated by Arild Emil Presthus as *Ludwig von Mises—Hans Liv Og Laere*. Printed in four parts in *Ideer om Frihet* (July 1981, pp. 15–18; Winter, 1982, pp. 12–15; Spring, 1982, pp. 19–21; and Winter, 1983, pp. 16–19). Translated by Jaoquín Reig as *Lo Esencial De Mises*. Madrid, Spain: Union Editorial, 1974.

SCHOLARLY ARTICLES & CHAPTERS IN BOOKS:

"Praxeology as the Method of Economics." Maurice Natanson, ed., *Phenomenology and the Social Sciences*. Evanston, Ill.: Northwestern University Press, 1973, pp. 311–39. Reprinted in *Austrian Economics*, vol. 1, by Stephen Littlechild, ed. Brookfield, Vt.: Edward Elgar, 1990, pp. 452–80. Reprinted excerpts in *Austrian Economics: A Reader* by Richard M. Ebeling, ed. Hillsdale, Mich.: Hillsdale

College Press, 1991, pp. 55–91. Reprinted in *The Logic of Action One: Method, Money, and the Austrian School*. Cheltenham, U.K.: Edward Elgar, 1997, pp. 28–57. Reprinted and expanded as *Economic Controversies*. Auburn, Ala.: Ludwig von Mises Institute, 2007.

"Praxeology as the Method of Social Sciences." *Individualism and the Social Sciences*. San Francisco: Cato Institute (Cato Paper, no. 4), 1979.

"Value Implications of Economic Theory." *The American Economist* (Spring, 1973): 35–39. Reprinted in *The Logic of Action One: Method, Money, and the Austrian School*. Cheltenham, U.K.: Edward Elgar, 1997, pp. 255–65. Reprinted and expanded as *Economic Controversies*. Auburn, Ala.: Ludwig von Mises Institute, 2007.

"Egalitarianism As a Revolt Against Nature." *Modern Age* (Fall, 1973): 348–57.

OTHER:

"The Sticks in the Closet," "The Editor Rebuts," "A Libertarian Poll," "Movement Magazines." *The Libertarian Forum* 5, no. 2 (1973).

"The Mayoral Circus." *The Libertarian Forum* 5, no. 3 (1973).

"The Apotheosis of Harry," "Sex Breaks up a Cult," "Arts and Movies," "Recommended Reading," "From the 'Old Curmudgeon'." *The Libertarian Forum* 5, no. 1 (January 1973).

"The New Isolationism." Interview with Rothbard and Leonard Liggio. *Reason* (February 1973): 4–19.

Review of *The Luddites*, by Malcolm I. Thomis. "The Original Machine-Haters." *Business and Society Review* (Spring, 1973): 110–12.

"Free Market, Police, Courts, and Law." *Reason* (March 1973): 5–19.

Review of *Revisionist Viewpoints: Essays in a Dissident Historical Tradition*, by James J. Martin. *Books for Libertarians* (March 1973): 4.

Review of *The Civilian and the Military*, by Arthur Ekirch, Jr. *Books for Libertarians* (March 1973): 4.

Review of *Germany Not Guilty in 1914*, by Michael H. Cochran. *Books for Libertarians* (March 1973 and May 1973).

Review of *In Quest of Truth and Justice*, by Harry Elmer Barnes. *Books for Libertarians* (March 1973 and May 1973).

Reviews of *The Twilight of Gold, 1914–1936: Myths and Realities*, by Melchior Palyi, and *The Monetary Sin of the West*, by Jacques Rueff. *Books for Libertarians* (March 1973 and May 1973).

"Present at the Creation," "Tax Rebellion," "Contra Psychological 'Liberation'," "Jim Davidson and the Week That Was," "Monthly Index of Liberty," "Recommended Reading." *The Libertarian Forum* 5, no. 4 (April 1973).

"The 'Counter Culture' Reveals Itself." *Human Events* (April 28, 1973): 18.

"Libertarian Strategy: A Reply to Mr. Katz." *New Libertarian Notes* (May 1973): 7.

"Notes on Watergate," "Floyd Arthur 'Baldy' Harper, RIP," "McGovern vs. Rothbard," "Arts and Movies," "Hospers on Rothbard's Rebuttal," "Recommended Reading," "The Editor's Final Rebuttal." *The Libertarian Forum* 5, no. 5 (May 1973).

"Will Rothbard's Free-Market Justice Suffice? Yes." *Reason* (May 1973): 19, 23–25.

"A Reply to McGovern." Letter to *Forum For Contemporary History*, 7 May 1973, p. 6.

Review of *The Conquest of Poverty*, by Henry Hazlitt. "A Perceptive Insight into Capitalism and the Welfare State," *Human Events* (May 19, 1973): 10.

Review of *Roads to Freedom: Essays in Honor of Friedrich A. von Hayek*, by Erich Streissler, Gottfried Habeler, Friedrich A. Lutz, and Fritz Machlup, eds. *Books for Libertarians* (June 1973).

"The Mayoral Circus, II," "The Editor Comments," "The Editor Rebuts," "The Need for a Movement and a Party," "Rothbardiana," "From the 'Old Curmudgeon'." *The Libertarian Forum* 5, no. 6 (June 1973).

"Interview: Rothbard Discusses Libertarianism." *The Stanford Daily*, 5 June 1973.

"Economic Mess," "Pareto on the Prospects for Liberty," "Arts and Movies." *The Libertarian Forum* 5, no. 7 (July 1973).

Review of *The Conquest of Poverty*, by Henry Hazlitt. *Books for Libertarians* (July 1973).

"101 Ways to Promote Libertarian Ideas," "Recommended Reading," "The Meaning of War." *The Libertarian Forum* 5, no. 8 (August 1973).

Review of *The Literature of Isolationism: A Guide To Non-Interventionist Scholarship 1930–1972*, by Justus Doenecke. *Books for Libertarians* (August 1973). The same review appeared in *Books for Libertarians* (December 1972).

Foreword to Walter Block's *Economic Scapegoats*. *New Libertarian Notes* (October 1973).

"Hands Off the Middle East!" "Send Money!" "The Libertarian: The Gospel According to Lefevre," "Revolution in Chile," "Arts and Movies." *The Libertarian Forum* 5, no. 10 (October 1973).

Review of *Liberty*, by Benjamin Tucker. *Books for Libertarians* (October 1973).

"Watergate, and the Argument From Knowledge." *Reason* (October 1973): 39.

"Ludwig von Mises: 1881–1973." *Human Events* (October 20, 1973): 7.

"Ludwig von Mises, RIP," "Libertarian Party," "From the 'Old Curmudgeon'," "Arts and Movies," "For Conspiracy Theorists Only!" *The Libertarian Forum* 5, no. 11 (November 1973).

Review of *Happy Days, Heathen Days, and Newspaper Days*, by H.L. Mencken. *Books for Libertarians* (November 1973).

"Congress, '73," "Rand on the Middle East." *The Libertarian Forum* 5, no. 12 (December 1973).

Review of *Dissent on Development*, by P.J. Baker. *Books for Libertarians* (December 1973): 1.

Review of *Economics*, by Paul A. Samuelson. *The Wall Street Review of Books* (December 1973): 518–22.

Reprinted as "Paul Samuelson's *Economics*, Ninth Edition" in *The Logic of Action Two: Applications and Criticism from the Austrian School*. Cheltenham, U.K.: Edward Elgar, 1997, pp. 254–59. Reprinted and expanded as *Economic Controversies*. Auburn, Ala.: Ludwig von Mises Institute, 2007.

"Revisionism and Libertarianism." *New Libertarian Notes*, 28 December 1973, pp. 7–8.

"City Prices Puzzle To Economists." Interview by Robert Lane, *New York Sunday News*, 17 June 1973, M11.

1974

BOOKS:

Egalitarianism As a Revolt Against Nature and Other Essays. Washington, D.C.: Libertarian Review Press, 1974. See article by this title (excluding "and Other Essays") in *Modern Age* (Fall, 1973): 348–57. Reprinted Auburn, Ala.: Ludwig von Mises Institute, 2000.

SCHOLARLY ARTICLES & CHAPTERS IN BOOKS:

"Historical Origins." William F. Rickenbacker, ed. *The Twelve Year Sentence*. La Salle, Ill.: Open Court Publishing, 1974, pp. 11–32.

"Justice and Property Rights." Samuel Blumenfeld, ed., *Property in a Humane Economy*. La Salle, Ill.: Open Court Publishing, 1974, pp. 101–22. Reprinted in *The Logic of Action One: Method, Money, and the Austrian School*. Cheltenham, U.K.: Edward Elgar, 1997, pp. 274–93. Reprinted and expanded as *Economic Controversies*. Auburn, Ala.: Ludwig von Mises Institute, 2007.

"Left and Right: The Prospects For Liberty." Tibor R. Machan, ed., *The Libertarian Alternative*. Chicago: Nelson-Hall, 1974, pp. 525–49. Originally appeared in *Left and Right* 1, no. 1 (Spring, 1965).

Review of *Competition and Entrepreneurship*, by Israel Kirzner. *Journal of Economic Literature* (1974): 902–03.

"The Anatomy of the State." Tibor R. Machan, ed., *The Libertarian Alternative*. Chicago: Nelson-Hall, 1974, pp. 69–93. Originally appeared in *Rampart Journal* (Summer, 1965): 1–24.

"The Importance of the Youngstein Campaign." Youngstein for Mayor, 1973, A Libertarian Campaign. New York: Adlib Communications, 1974, p. 5.

"Why Inflation Must Lead to Recession or Depression." Louis E. Carabini, ed., *Everything You Need To Know About Gold and Silver*. New Rochelle, N.Y.: Arlington House, 1974, pp. 11–32. Originally appeared in *Pacific Coast Coin Exchange Gold & Silver Newsletter*, 30 November 1972.

Review of *The Twisted Dream*, by Douglas Dowd. *Business History Review* (Winter, 1974).

OTHER:

"Energy Fascism," "Danish Delight," "Arts and Movies." *The Libertarian Forum* 6, no. 1 (January 1974).

"Privacy, Or the 'Right To Know'?" *Reason* (January 1974): 28, 30.

Review of *The Strike-Threat System*, by William H. Hutt. *Books for Libertarians* (January 1974).

Review of *The Collected Works of Lysander Spooner*, by Lysander Spooner. *Books for Libertarians* (February 1974).

"Two Tiers Crumble?" "Relevance?" "What Kind of 'Purity'?" "An Open Letter to Irving Kristol," "Political Kidnapping," "Rothbardiana," "Arts and Movies," "Save the Oil Industry!" "New Associates," "101 Ways to Promote Libertarian Ideas." *The Libertarian Forum* 6, no. 2 (February 1974).

Review of *Social Darwinism: Selected Essays*, by William Graham Sumner. *Books for Libertarians* (March 1974): 5.

Review of *The Unheavenly City*, by Edward Banfield. *Books for Libertarians* (March 1974): 1.

Reviews of *Our Enemy, the State*, by Albert J. Nock, and *As We Go Marching*, by John T. Flynn. "Two Libertarian Classics." *Reason* (March 1974): 10–11.

"Seven Days in May?" "The British Elections," "Why No Oil Refineries?" "How to Deal With Kidnapping?" "Libertarian Songs–I," "Libertarian Songs–II," "Libertarian Dinner Club," "Civil Liberties, Selective Style." *The Libertarian Forum* 6, no. 3 (March 1974).

"Five Years Old!" "FLP Convention: One Step Forward, One Step Back," "The Mysterious World of the CIA," "Phillip H. Wilkie, RIP," "Arts and Movies," "Apologies!" *The Libertarian Forum* 6, no. 4 (April 1974).

"Law Without Government." *Reason* (April 1974): 40.

Reviews of *The Inevitability of Patriarchy*, by Steven Goldberg, and *Sexual Suicide*, by George Gilder. *Books for Libertarians* (April 1974): 1, 9.

"Impeach the . . . (Expletive Deleted)," "BFL Expands," "Uncle Miltie Rides Again," "Purity and the Libertarian Party." *The Libertarian Forum* 6, no. 5 (May 1974).

Review of *As We Go Marching*, by John T. Flynn. *Books for Libertarians* (May 1974): 9.

"Dr. Rothbard Replies." *Books for Libertarians* (June 1974): 23. Re: Rothbard's review of *The Inevitability of Patriarchy* by Steven Goldberg.

"Reflections on the Middle East," "Arts and Movies," "For Kurdistan," "The Hiss Case Revisited," "From the 'Old Curmudgeon'," "Obit Note." *The Libertarian Forum* 6, no. 6 (June 1974).

Review of *Three Sacred Cows of Economics*, by A. Rubner. *Books for Libertarians* (June 1974): 4. "The Movie Hero Is a Vital Part of American Culture." *Human Events* (June 15, 1974): 16.

"Deflation Or More Inflation?" *Inflation Survival Letter*, 17 June 1974, p. 49.

Hatred of the Automobile." *Reason* (July 1974): 34.

"Scarcity Vs. Shortage." *Skeptic* (July 1974): 10–11.

"The American Revolution Reconsidered." *Books for Libertarians* (July 1974): 6–7.

"World-Wide Inflation," "New Forum Policy," "Revisionist Seminar," "New Rothbard Book." *The Libertarian Forum* 6, no. 7 (July 1974).

"The Austrian School's Advice: 'Hands Off'!" Article based on interviews with Rothbard and other Austrian economists. *Business Week*, 3 August 1974, pp. 40–41.

"Whoopee!!" "Kennedy Marriage Revisionism," "Libertarian Advance," "From the 'Old Curmudgeon'," "Recommended Reading," "Arts and Movies." *The Libertarian Forum* 6, no. 8 (August 1974).

"Only One Heartbeat Away," "Correction." *The Libertarian Forum* 6, no. 9 (September 1974).

"Nobel Prize." *The Libertarian Forum* 6, no. 10 (October 1974).

"The Greenspan Nomination." *Reason* (October 1974): 39.

"Henry Hazlitt Celebrates 80th Birthday." *Human Events* (November 1974): 8.

"The Elections," "Voting and Politics," "After Rabat, What?" "Economic Determinism, Ideology, and the American Revolution," "Report from Europe," "Note to our Readers." *The Libertarian Forum* 6, no. 11 (November 1974).

"Conservatives Gratified By Nobel Prize To Von Hayek." *Human Events* (November 16, 1974): 18.

"The Emerging Crisis," "Libertarian Scholarship Advances," "Boston Libertarian Dinners!" "Henry Hazlitt Celebrates 80th Birthday," "Arts and Movies." *The Libertarian Forum* 6, no. 12 (December 1974).

1975

BOOKS:

Conceived in Liberty, vol. I: *A New Land, A New People, The American Colonies in the Seventeenth Century*. New Rochelle, N.Y.: Arlington House Publishers, 1975. (With the assistance of Leonard P. Liggio.)

Conceived in Liberty, vol. II: *"Salutary Neglect": The American Colonies in the First Half of the Eighteenth Century*. New Rochelle, N.Y.: Arlington House Publishers, 1975.

SCHOLARLY ARTICLES & CHAPTERS IN BOOKS:

"Gold vs. Fluctuating Fiat Exchange Rates." Hans F. Sennholz, ed., *Gold is Money*, Westport, Conn.: Greenwood Press, 1975, pp. 24–40. Reprinted in *The Logic of Action One: Method, Money, and the Austrian School*. Cheltenham, U.K.: Edward Elgar, 1997, pp. 350–63. Reprinted and expanded as *Economic Controversies*. Auburn, Ala.: Ludwig von Mises Institute, 2007.

"Justice and Property Rights." Samuel Blumenfeld, ed., *Property in a Humane Economy*. Champaign, Ill.: Open Court, 1975.

"Total Reform: Nothing Less." E.G. West, ed., *Nonpublic School Aid*. Lexington, Mass.: Lexington Books, 1975, pp. 102–07.

OTHER:

Introduction to *The Politics of Obedience, The Discourse of Voluntary Servitude: The Political Thought of Étienne de la Boétie*. New York: Free Life Editions, 1975, pp. 9–42.

"Government and the Economy," "Society Without a State," "New Rothbard Books!" *The Libertarian Forum* 7, no. 1 (January 1975).

"Semantic Trickery and Economic Health." *Reason* (January 1975): 47.

"Oil War and Oil Imperialism" (section 2 by Joseph R. Stromberg; section 3 by Rep. Howard H. Buffet), "Tax Rebellion in Willimantic," "The Day-Care Shortage," "Sense on Oil–At Last!" *The Libertarian Forum* 7, no. 2 (February 1975).

Review of *An Objective Theory of Probability*, by Donald Gillies. *The Libertarian Review* (February 1975): 9.

"Inflationary Depression," "Arts and Movies," "Under-Population?" "Spring, Books." *The Libertarian Forum* 7, no. 3 (March 1975).

"Getting At the Roots of Inflation." *Libertarian Party News*, March-April 1975, p. 3.

"The Death of a State," "LP Convention," "Come One, Come All!" "Nozick Award," "Assassination Revisionism Once More," "Arts and Movies." *The Libertarian Forum* 7, no. 4 (April 1975).

"The Oil Caper." *Reason* (April 1975): 39.

"Mayaguez, By Jingo," "Libertarian Ripoff of the Month." *The Libertarian Forum* 7, no. 5 (May 1975).

Review of *Building the Organizational Society*, by J. Israel, ed. *The Libertarian Review* (June 1975): 8–9. (Unsigned)

Reviews of *Omnipotent Government and Theory and History*, by Ludwig von Mises. *The Libertarian Review* (June 1975): 1.

"Saving Yourself By Saving Freedom." *Reason* (June 1975): 60–63.

"The Case for Optimism," "The Bankruptcy of Liberalism," "Recommended Reading: Hayek Interview," "The Ethics Gap." *The Libertarian Forum* 7, no. 6 (June 1975).

"Inflation Or Deflation." *Inflation Survival Letter*, 4 June 1975, pp. 87–89.

"Dictatorships," "From the 'Old Curmudgeon'." *The Libertarian Forum* 7, no. 7 (July 1975).

"The Death of a State—1." *Reason* (July 1975): 31–32.

Reviews of *Herbert Spencer: Structure, Function and Evolution*, by Stanislav Andreski, ed., and *Herbert Spencer: The Evolution of a Sociologist*, by J.D.Y. Peel. *The Libertarian Review* (August 1975): 2.

Review of *The State*, by Franz Oppenheimer. *The Libertarian Review* (September 1975): 1.

"The LP Convention," "All Founded," "Rothbardiana," "Recommended Reading." *The Libertarian Forum* 8, no. 9 (September 1975).

"Rothbard: Timing Is Right For Concerted LP Efforts." *Libertarian Party News*, September-October 1975, pp. 6–7.

"The Reign of Dictatorships." *Reason* (October 1975): 33–34.

"The Sinai Trap," "Arab Wars," "Arts and Movies," "From the 'Old Curmudgeon'." *The Libertarian Forum* 8, no. 10 (October 1975).

"Politics: November '75," "New Associates." *The Libertarian Forum* 8, no. 11 (November 1975).

Review of *Growth of the American Revolution*, by Bernhard Knollenberg. *The Libertarian Review* (November 1975): 2.

Review of *The World Between the Wars*, by Joseph S. Davis. *The Libertarian Review* (December 1975).

1976

BOOKS:

Conceived in Liberty, vol. III: *Advance to Revolution 1760–1784*. New Rochelle, N.Y.: Arlington House Publishers, 1976.

SCHOLARLY ARTICLES & CHAPTERS IN BOOKS:

"Deflation Reconsidered." Peter Corbin and Murray Sabrin, eds., *Geographical Aspects of Inflationary Processes*, vol. I. Pleasantville, N.Y.: Redgrave Publishing, 1976.

"Ludwig von Mises and Economic Calculation Under Socialism." Laurence Moss, ed., *The Economics of Ludwig von Mises*. Kansas City: Sheed and Ward, 1976, pp. 67–77. Reprinted in *The Logic of Action One: Method, Money, and the Austrian School*. Cheltenham, U.K.: Edward Elgar, 1997, pp. 397–407. Reprinted and expanded as *Economic Controversies*. Auburn, Ala.: Ludwig von Mises Institute, 2007.

"New Light on the Prehistory of the Austrian School." Edwin G. Dolan, ed., *The Foundations of Modern Austrian Economics*. Kansas City: Sheed and Ward, 1976, pp. 52–74. *The Logic of Action One: Method, Money, and the Austrian School*. Cheltenham, U.K.: Edward Elgar, 1997, pp. 173–94. Reprinted and expanded as *Economic Controversies*. Auburn, Ala.: Ludwig von Mises Institute, 2007.

"Praxeology: The Methodology of Austrian Economics." Edwin G. Dolan, ed., *The Foundations of Modern Austrian Economics*. Kansas City: Sheed and Ward, 1976, pp. 19–39. Reprinted in *The Logic of Action One: Method, Money, and the Austrian School*. Cheltenham, U.K.: Edward Elgar, 1997, pp. 58–77. Reprinted and expanded as *Economic Controversies*. Auburn, Ala.: Ludwig von Mises Institute, 2007.

"Praxeology, Value Judgments, and Public Policy." Edwin G. Dolan, ed., *The Foundations of Modern Austrian Economics*. Kansas City: Sheed and Ward, 1976, pp. 89–111. Reprinted in *The Logic of Action One: Method, Money, and the Austrian School*. Cheltenham, U.K.: Edward Elgar, 1997, pp. 78–99. Reprinted and expanded as *Economic Controversies*. Auburn, Ala.: Ludwig von Mises Institute, 2007.

"The Austrian Theory of Money." Edwin G. Dolan, ed., *The Foundations of Modern Austrian Economics*. Kansas City: Sheed and Ward, 1976, pp. 160–84. Reprinted in *The Logic of Action One: Method, Money, and the Austrian School*. Cheltenham, U.K.: Edward Elgar, 1997, pp. 297–320. Reprinted and expanded as *Economic Controversies*. Auburn, Ala.: Ludwig von Mises Institute, 2007.

"The New Deal and the International Monetary System." Leonard Liggio and James Martin, eds., *Watershed of Empire: Essays on New Deal Foreign Policy*. Colorado Springs, Colo.: Ralph Myles, 1976, pp. 19–64. Reprinted in Garet Garrett and Rothbard, *The Great Depression and New Deal Monetary Policy*. San Francisco, Calif.: Cato Institute (Cato Paper, no. 13), 1980, pp. 79–124.

OTHER:

Foreword to *Defending the Undefendable*, by Walter Block. New York: Fleet Press, 1976, pp. 7–9.

"Default Now!" *Reason* (January 1976): 33.

"U.S. Out of Angola!," "MacBride vs. Reagan," "The ABM Slips Away," "Libertarian Bicentennial," "Arts and Movies," "Free Doug Kennell!" "Libertarian Environmentalists." *The Libertarian Forum* 9, no. 1 (January 1976).

"The Presidency '76, the Morning Line," "We Make the Media!" "Revisionism and Libertarianism," "Center for Libertarian Studies Formed!" "Von Hoffman versus Schlesinger." *The Libertarian Forum* 9, no. 2 (February 1976).

"The Early Primaries," "Libertarian Feminists Organize," "African Roundup," "The Lebanon Tragedy." *The Libertarian Forum* 9, no. 3 (March 1976).

"FLP Split!" "Statement," "A Political Party, Once More," "Combating Conservatism," "The 'Defense Gap' Mythology." *The Libertarian Forum* 9, no. 4 (April 1976).

"Free Market Economics Can Be Fun." *Fortune* (April 1976): 167–68.

"The Angola Caper." *Reason* (April 1976): 39.

"The Zen Candidate, or, Browning Out in the Movement," "On Nozick's Anarchy, State and Utopia–II," "Arts and Movies." *The Libertarian Forum* 9, no. 5 (May 1976).

"Inflation: Its Cause and Cure." Libertarian Party position paper #2, no date. Reprinted in *Inflation Survival Letter*, 19 May 1976, pp. 148, 157.

"The Man Who Would Be King." *The Libertarian Review* (May-June 1976): 9–15.

"Ford vs. Carter?" "Who's Behind . . . ?" "The Psycho-Presidency?" *The Libertarian Forum* 9, no. 6 (June 1976).

"America's Libertarian Revolution." *Reason* (July 1976): 39–43.

"MacBride's New Book," "News From Spain," "CLS Booms!" "Democratic Convention Notes," "Arts and Movies." *The Libertarian Forum* 9, no. 7 (July 1976).

"The Panama Canal Caper." *Reason* (July 1976): 45, 55.

"Thinking About Revolution." *The Libertarian Forum* 9, no. 9 (September 1976).

"Interview: Murray Rothbard." *Penthouse* (October 1976): 116–18, 173–78.

"The Danger of Opportunism." *Reason* (October 1976): 39.

"To the Elections," "The LP Convention," "Benediction's Speech at the LP Convention," "Storm Over the 'Scum': Defending the Undefendable Block," "Recommended Reading." *The Libertarian Forum* 9, no. 10 (October 1976).

"The LP: Retrospect and Prospect," "Metric Mania." *The Libertarian Forum* 9, no. 11 (November 1976).

"Carter & Co.–Back At the Old Stand," "Nobel Prize for Friedman," "From the 'Old Curmudgeon'," "New Libertarian Scholarly Journal." *The Libertarian Forum* 9, no. 12 (December 1976).

"The Human Side of Von Mises." Review of *My Years With Ludwig von Mises*, by Margit von Mises. *Human Events* (December 25, 1976): 988–89.

1977

SCHOLARLY ARTICLES & CHAPTERS IN BOOKS:

"Punishment and Proportionality." Randy E. Barnett and John Hagel, III, eds., *Assessing the Criminal: Restitution, Retribution, and the Legal Process.* Cambridge, Mass.: Ballinger Publishing , 1977, pp. 259–70.

"Editorial." *Journal of Libertarian Studies* 1, no. 1 (Winter, 1977): 1.

Review of *Business Ideologies in the Reform-Progressive Era*, by Alfred Thimm. *Journal of Economic History* (September 1977).

OTHER:

Introduction to *Capital, Interest, and Rent: Essays in the Theory of Distribution*, by Frank A. Fetter. Kansas City: Sheed Andrews and McMeel, 1977, pp. 1–23. Preface to the same, internally dated March 1976.

Introduction to *Lysander Spooner: Libertarian Pietist, Vices Are Not Crimes.* Cupertino, Calif.: Tanstaafl, 1977, pp. xiii–xvii.

Review of *Gold, Money and the Law*, by Henry G. Manne and Roger L. Miller, eds. *Law and Liberty Newsletter*, Winter, 1977, pp. 8–9. Law and Liberty Project of the Institute for Humane Studies.

"LP Election Scoreboard," "More on Carter & Co.," "Arts and Movies," "Land Reform: Portugal and Mexico," "Relaxation in China," "Vive Le Quebec Libre." *The Libertarian Forum* 10, no. 1 (January 1977).

"The Achievement of the LP." *Reason* (January 1977).

"WMA Interview: Murray N. Rothbard." *World Money Analyst*, January 1977, pp. 8–10.

Review of *My Years With Ludwig von Mises*, by Margit von Mises. *The Libertarian Review* (January-February, 1977): 4.

"The War Over Foreign Policy," "Recommended Reading," "One Man Against OSHA," "From the 'Old Curmudgeon'," "The Natural Gas Caper," "Arts and Movies." *The Libertarian Forum* 10, no. 2 (February 1977).

"Errata," "A Great Day for Freedom," "From the 'Old Curmudgeon'," "Kidnappers At Large," "American and 'Human Rights'–East Timor Division," "Arts and Movies," "Zaire–Katanga Rises Again!" *The Libertarian Forum* 10, no. 3 (March 1977).

"Revenues and Other Thugs." *Skeptic* (March-April 1977): 34–37, 60–61.

"At the Summit," "The Death of General Hershey," "The Great Felkner Caper," "The Historians' Betrayal," "The Tuccille Defection," "Arts and Movies." *The Libertarian Forum* 10, no. 4 (April 1977).

"The Conspiracy Theory of History Revisited." *Reason* (April 1977): 39–40.

"Defending Economism." Correspondence to *Reason* (June 1977): 13.

"Carter's Energy Fascism: Prescription For Power." *The Libertarian Review* (July 1977): 10–13, 46.

"Reagan Watch." *The Libertarian Review* (August 1977): 10–12.

"The Myth of Democratic Socialism." *The Libertarian Review* (September 1977): 24–27, 45.

"Demagoguery at the White House." *The Wall Street Journal*, 3 November, 1977, p. 16. A full page statement by economists for responsible energy policy. Signed by Rothbard, among others.

"The Treaty That Wall Street Wrote." *Inquiry* (December 5, 1977): 9–14.

1978

Scholarly Articles & Chapters in Books:

"Austrian Definitions of the Supply of Money." Louis Spadaro, ed., *New Directions in Austrian Economics*. Kansas City: Sheed Andrews and McMeel, 1978, pp. 143–56. Reprinted in *The Logic of Action One: Method, Money, and the Austrian School*. Cheltenham, U.K.: Edward Elgar, 1997, pp. 337–49. Reprinted and expanded as *Economic Controversies*. Auburn, Ala.: Ludwig von Mises Institute, 2007.

"Freedom, Inequality, Primitivism and the Division of Labor." Kenneth Templeton, ed., *The Politicalization of Society*. Indianapolis, Ind.: Liberty Press, 1978, pp. 83–126. Originally appeared in *Modern Age* (Summer, 1971).

"Society Without a State." J. Roland Pennock and John W. Chapman, eds. *Anarchism: Nomos* XIX. New York: New York University Press, 1978, pp. 191–207. Originally appeared in *The Libertarian Forum* (January 1975): 3–7. Reprinted in Tibor R. Machan, *The Libertarian Reader*. Totowa, N.J.: Rowman and Littlefield, 1982, pp. 53–63.

"The Foreign Policy of the Old Right." *Journal of Libertarian Studies* 2, no. 1 (Winter, 1978): 85–96.

Other:

"The Tarring and Feathering of John Kenneth Galbraith." *The Mercury* (January 1978): 25–32.

Reviews of *The International Monetary System, 1945–1976*, by Robert Solomon, and *The Origins of the International Economic Disorder*, by Fred L. Block. "Monetary Nonsense," *Inquiry* (January 2, 1978): 26–27.

"Thoughts On Coalitions and Alignments." *Libertarian Party News*, January-February 1978, p. 3. Reprinted as "On Coalitions and Alignments" in *Common Sense* (January-February 1983).

"The Last Word on Efronia." *The Libertarian Forum* 11, no. 1 (January-February 1978).

"Modern Historians Confront the American Revolution." *Literature of Liberty* (January-March 1978): 16–41.

"Strengthening the LP," "Assassination Revisionism," "Arts and Movies." *The Libertarian Forum* 11, no. 2 (March-April 1978).

"Cloning: Menace Or Promise?" *The Libertarian Review* (April 1978): 7.

Review of *Notes and Recollections*, by Ludwig von Mises. "The Mises We Never Knew," *The Libertarian Review* (April 1978): 37–38.

"So What Else Is New?" *The Libertarian Review* (April 1978): 9.

"Soviet Foreign Policy: A Revisionist Perspective." *The Libertarian Review* (April 1978): 23–27.

"Out of the Living Room." *Reason* (May 1978): 36–37.

"The Efron Affair." *The Libertarian Review* (May 1978): 14–15.

"Victory for Tax Revolt!" "Arts and Movies." *The Libertarian Forum* 11, no. 3 (May-June 1978).

"The Capital Punishment Question." *The Libertarian Review* (June 1978): 13–14.

"The Kondratieff Cycle Myth." *Inflation Survival Letter.*

"Getting Tough in Zaire." *The Libertarian Review* (July 1978): 10–11.

"Strategies For a Libertarian Victory." *The Libertarian Review* (August 1978): 18–24, 34.

"The Tax Revolt." *Reason* (September 1978): 39, 47.

"Lessons of the People's Temple," "Newsletters of Libertarian Interest." *The Libertarian Forum* 11, no. 5 (September-October 1978).

"Camp David and After." *The Libertarian Review* (October 1978): 14–16.

Reviews of *The Inflation Crisis And How To Resolve It*, by Henry Hazlitt and *Beyond Boom and Crash*, by Robert Heilbroner, and *Manias, Panics, and Crashes*, by Charles Kindleberger. "Boom! Crack! Crash!" *Inquiry* (October 30, 1978): 21–22.

"Free Or Compulsory Speech." *The Libertarian Review* (November 1978): 11–12.

"LP Breakthrough." *The Libertarian Forum* 11, no. 6 (November-December 1978).

"Optimism and Pessimism in Hong Kong." *Reason* (December 1978): 50, 54.

"The Breakthrough Election." *The Libertarian Review* (December 1978): 12–13.

Review of *Can Government Go Bankrupt?* by Richard Rose and Guy Peters. "Saving the State From Itself." *Inquiry* (December 11, 1978): 17–18.

1979

BOOKS:

Conceived in Liberty, vol. IV: *The Revolutionary War 1775–1784*. New Rochelle, N.Y.: Arlington House Publishers, 1979.

Individualism and the Philosophy of the Social Sciences. San Francisco: Cato Institute (Cato Paper, no. 4), 1979. Includes "The Mantle of Science" (1960) and "Praxeology as the Method of the Social Sciences" (1973). These two papers were translated in French as "Les oripeaux de la science" and "La praxeologie comme methode des sciences sociales" by François Guillaumat in *Economistses et charlatans*. Paris: Les Belles Lettres, 1991, pp. 1–38 and pp. 39–81.

SCHOLARLY ARTICLES & CHAPTERS IN BOOKS:

"Hoover's 1919 Food Diplomacy in Retrospect." Lawrence E. Gelfand, ed., *Herbert Hoover: The Great War and its Aftermath, 1914–1923*. Iowa City: University of Iowa Press, 1979.

"The Myth of Efficiency." Mario J. Rizzo, ed., *Time, Uncertainty, and Disequilibrium*. Lexington, Mass.: Lexington Books, 1979, pp. 90–95. Translated in French as "Le mythe de l'efficience" by François Guillaumat in *Economistes et charlatans*. Paris: Les Belles Lettres, 1991, pp. 178–94. Reprinted in *The Logic of Action One: Method, Money, and the Austrian School*. Cheltenham, U.K.: Edward Elgar, 1997, pp. 266–73. Reprinted and expanded as *Economic Controversies*. Auburn, Ala.: Ludwig von Mises Institute, 2007.

OTHER:

"Statism, Left, Right and Center." *The Libertarian Review* (January 1979): 14–15.

"Rothbard Replies 1." *The Libertarian Review* (January 1979): 10. Re: Robert Nozick's letter on Anwar Sadat; Rothbard replies to Nozick's criticism that he, Rothbard, is more anti-Zionist than Sadat.

"Rothbard Replies 2." *The Libertarian Review* (January 1979): 11. Re: T. Fressolis's letter on capital punishment.

"The Space War" (With Rick White, Ed Crane, and Tonie Nathan). *The Libertarian Forum* 12, no. 1 (January-February 1979).

Review of *Welfare*, by Martin Anderson. *Reason* (February 1979): 41–42.

"The Menace of the Space Cult." *The Libertarian Review* (February 1979): 14–15.

"The Myth of Monolithic Communism." *Libertarian Review* (February 1979): 32–35.

Review of *A Dangerous Place*, by Daniel P. Moynihan. "Bill and Irving and Ken and Patrick," *Inquiry* (February 5, 1979): 21–23.

"1978—The Breakthrough Year." *Reason* (March 1979): 9–40, 49.

"The Meaning of San Jose." *The Libertarian Review* (March 1979): 20–21.

"The Ten Most Dangerous Economic Fallacies of Our Time." *Personal Finance* (March 21, 1979): 65–68.

Ten Years Old!" *The Libertarian Forum* 12, no. 2 (March-April 1979).

"The First New Dealer." Review of *Herbert Hoover: A Public Life* by David Burner. *Inquiry* (April 16, 1979): 21–23.

"Scholasticism and Austrian Economics." *Literature of Liberty* (April-June 1979): 78–79.

"The Balanced Budget Question." *The Libertarian Review* (May 1979): 23.

"Listen Again, YAF!" "Libertarians on the Battlements," "'S Wonderful, 'S Wonderful," "LP Radical Caucus Formed." *Libertarian Forum* 12, no. 3 (May-June 1979).

"Rothbard Replies 3." *The Libertarian Review* (June 1979): 15. Re: Tibor R. Machan's letter to the editor.

"The Death of a State." *Reason* (June 1979): 53, 58.

"Nuclear Power Crisis," "Late Bulletin: SLS Makes Threats!" "Technological Facts on Nuclear Energy," "Late Bulletin: LR Suppresses Free and Open Debate on Nuclear Power!" *The Libertarian Forum* 12, no. 4 (July-August 1979).

"The Gas 'Shortage'." *The Libertarian Review* (July-August 1979): 15–16.

"*National Review* and the Pro-Government Coalition." *Reason* (September 1979): 42–43.

"The Iran Threat." *The Libertarian Forum* 12, no. 5 (September-October 1979).

"To Nuke or Not to Nuke." *The Libertarian Review* (October 1979): 9.

"Reliving the Crash of '29." *Inquiry* (November 12, 1979): 15–19.

"The Evil of Banality." Review of *Breaking Ranks*, by Norman Podhoretz. *Inquiry* (December 10, 1979): 26–28.

"Street Action in Gotham." *Inquiry* (December 24, 1979): 9.

"The Threatening Economy." *The New York Times Magazine*, 30 December 1979, pp. 12–15, 33–35. Interview with Rothbard by David Mermelstein begins at p. 15.

1980

SCHOLARLY ARTICLES & CHAPTERS IN BOOKS:

"Myths and Truths About Libertarianism." *Modern Age* (Winter, 1980): 9–15. Reprinted as "The Ethics of Freedom." *Free Texas* (Spring, 1981): 3.

"King on Punishment: A Comment." *Journal of Libertarian Studies* 4, no. 2 (Spring, 1980): 167–72.

"Ludwig von Mises and Natural Law: A Comment on Professor Gonce." *Journal of Libertarian Studies* 4, no. 3 (Summer, 1980): 289–97.

Review of *A Theory of Capitalist Regulation: The U.S. Experience*, by Michel Aglietta. *Journal of Economic History* (June 1980).

OTHER:

Foreword to *Economic Forecasting— Models or Markets?* by James Bernard Ramsey. San Francisco: Cato Institute, 1980, pp. ix–xii. Cato Paper, no. 10, internally dated August 1980.

Foreword to Ludwig von Mises, *The Theory of Money and Credit*. Indianapolis: Liberty*Classics*, 1980, pp. 13–16.

"Hayek On Coercion and Freedom." *Literature of Liberty* (Winter, 1980): 53–54.

"And Now, Afghanistan," "Notes on Iran, Afghanistan, etc." *The Libertarian Forum* 13, no. 1 (January-February 1980).

"The Importance of the Caucus." *Libertarian Party News*, January-February 1980, pp. 3, 7.

"Stateless Defense of Rights." *Literature of Liberty* (Spring, 1980): 61.

"Collective Guilt in Iran." *Reason* (March 1980): 47–48.

"The Presidential Campaign: The Need for Radicalism." *The Libertarian Forum* 13, no. 2 (March-April 1980).

"Opportunism, Nukes, and the Clark Campaign," "Fired From LR," "Evers for Congress." *The Libertarian Forum* 13, no. 3 (May-June 1980).

Review of *Research in Economic History*, by Paul Uselding, ed. *Business History Review* (Summer, 1980).

"Carter, Pain, and Inflation." *Reason* (June, 1980): 61–62.

"Interview 1: Murray Rothbard." *Toward Liberty* (Toronto), June 1980, pp. 1–2, 4.

Review of *World War I and the Origins of Civil Liberties in the United States*, by Paul Murphy. *Inquiry* (June 9, 1980): 22–24.

"The Two Faces of Ronald Reagan." *Inquiry* (July 7, 1980): 16–20.

"Ethnic Politics in New York," "Is It Legal to Treat Sick Birds?" "Free-Market Congressman in Action?" "Bloated and Swollen." *The Libertarian Forum* 13, no. 4 (July-August 1980).

"Libertarianism Versus 'Low Tax Liberalism'." *Cadre* (the internal bulletin of the Libertarian Party Radical Caucus; July-August, 1980): 1–3.

"Mises's Regression Theorem." *The Essence*, Series 5 (Institute for Humane Studies, Menlo Park, Calif.), August-November 1980.

"Stereotypes Live!" *Reason* (September 1980): 54–55.

"The Clark Campaign: Never Again," "Arts and Movies." *The Libertarian Forum* 13, nos. 5–6 (September-December 1980).

"Requiem For the Old Right." Review of *The Odyssey of the American Right*, by Michael W. Miles. *Inquiry* (October 27, 1980): 24–27.

"Frank Chodorov: Individualist." *Fragments* (January-March 1967): 13. Reprinted in *Fragments* (October-December 1980): 11.

"From Cuban To American Socialism." *Reason* (December 1980): 60.

1981

SCHOLARLY ARTICLES & CHAPTERS IN BOOKS:

Review of *The Political Economy of the Educational Process*, by Richard B. McKenzie. *Southern Economic Journal* (April 1981).

"The Laissez-Faire Radical.: A Quest for the Historical Mises." *Journal of Libertarian Studies* 5, no. 3 (Summer, 1981): 237–53.

"Frank S. Meyer: Fusionist As Libertarian Manque." *Modern Age* (Fall, 1981): 352–63.

"The Myth of Neutral Taxation." *The Cato Journal* 1, no. 2 (Fall, 1981): 519–64. Reprinted in *The Logic of Action Two: Applications and Criticism from the Austrian School*. Cheltenham, U.K.: Edward Elgar, 1997, pp. 56–108. Reprinted and expanded as *Economic Controversies*. Auburn, Ala.: Ludwig von Mises Institute, 2007.

OTHER:

Foreword to Ludwig von Mises, *The Theory of Money and Credit*. Indianapolis: Liberty*Classics*, 1981, pp. 13–16.

"It Usually Ends With Ed Crane," "The War for the Soul of the Party." *The Libertarian Forum* 14, nos. 1–2 (January-April 1981).

"Left-Opportunism: The Case of SLS." *Libertarian Vanguard* (February-March 1981): 10–12.

Interview with Murray Rothbard, *Hard Money News* (Spring, 1981): 7, 15–19.

"The Election: The Case For Pessimism." *Reason* (March 1981): 46.

"The Reagan Budget—An Open Letter To President Reagan." *International Moneyline* (March 1981): 8–10.

Interview with Rothbard. *Silver & Gold Report* 6, no. 6 (Late March 1981): 1–6.

"Taxation: Is It Voluntary?" *Libertarian Party News*, March-April 1981, pp. 13–15.

"Felix the Fixer To the Rescue." *Inquiry* (April 27, 1981): 7–10.

"Konkin On Libertarian Strategy." *Strategy of the New Libertarian Alliance* 1 (May 1981): 3–11. Reprinted as "The Anti-Party Mentality" in *Libertarian Vanguard* (August-September, 1981): 17.

"The Importance of the LP Platform." *Libertarian Party News* (May-June 1981): 2, 19.

Foreword to *Government's Money Monopoly*, by Henry Mark Holzer, ed. New York: Books in Focus, 1981, pp. ix–x.

"It Usually Ends With Ed Crane." *Libertarian Vanguard* (June 1981): 18–19.

"The Reagan Fraud." *Reason* (June 1981): 84. Translated by A.E. Presthus as "Reagan's Bloff." *Ideer Om Frihet* 3, no. 1 (Winter, 1982): 18–19.

"Left-Opportunism: The Case of SLS, Part II." *Libertarian Vanguard* (June 1981): 16–17, 23.

Review of *The Speculator: Bernard M. Baruch in Washington*, by J. Schwarz. "Wheels Within Wheels." *Inquiry* (June 15, 29, 1981): 22–24.

"Crane/Cato Once More: Part I–An Open Letter to the Crane Machine," "Catogate: Who's the Mole (or Moles) at Cato?" "Hallmark of a Free Society." *The Libertarian Forum* 15, nos. 3–4 (June-July 1981).

"Big News! Lib. Forum Reorganized!" "LP/10: A Mixed Bag," "The Kochtopus: Convulsions and Contradictions," "Hayek's Denationalised Money," "Against a Government Space Program," "Errata," "Consolation for Activists." *The Libertarian Forum* 15, nos. 5–6 (August 1981– January 1982).

"O Que E Anarco-Capitalismo?" *Visao Magazine* (Sao Paula, Brazil), 10 August 1981, pp. 62–65.

"Freedom Faces Risky Future." *Free Texas* (Fall, 1981): 1, 11.

"Politics of Principle." Letter to *Free Texas* 10, no. 4 (Fall, 1981): 23.

"The Moral Majority and the Public Schools." *Reason* (September 1981): 46.

"P.T. Barnum Was Right." *Inquiry* (May 25, 1981): 19–21. Reprinted in the "Economic Outlook" column of *Mother Earth News* 71 (September-October, 1981): 28–29.

"Murray Rothbard on the New York City Mayoral Campaign." Advertisement for Judith Jones, Libertarian for Mayor. Broadside Letter, October 1981, p. 1.

Review of *The Last Laugh*, by Sidney J. Perelman. "Notes From Namlerep." *Inquiry* (October 19, 1981): 28–29.

"Reagan and King Canute." *Reason* (December 1981): 65.

1982

BOOKS:

The Ethics of Liberty. Atlantic Highlands, N.J.: Humanities Press, 1982. Translated in French by François Guillaumat as *L'éthique de la liberté*. Paris: Les Belles Lettres, 1991. Translated in Spanish by Marciano Villanueva Salas as *La Etica de la Libertad*. Madrid: Union Editorial, 1995. Translated in Italian by L. Marco Bassani as *L'etica della libertà*. Macerata: Liberilibri di AMA srl, 1996. Reissued with new introduction by Hans-Hermann Hoppe. New York: New York University Press, 1998.

SCHOLARLY ARTICLES & CHAPTERS IN BOOKS:

"Interventionism: Comment on Lavoie." Israel Kirzner, ed., *Method, Process, and Austrian Economics*. Lexington, Mass.: Lexington Books, 1982, pp. 185–88.

"Law, Property Rights, and Air Pollution." *Cato Journal* 2, no. 1 (Spring, 1982): 55–99. Reprinted in *The Logic of Action Two: Applications and Criticism from the Austrian School*. Cheltenham, U.K.: Edward Elgar, 1997, pp. 121–70. Reprinted and expanded as *Economic Controversies*. Auburn, Ala.: Ludwig von Mises Institute, 2007.

OTHER:

"Are We Being Beastly to the Gipper? Part I," "This the Movement You Have Chosen," "Arts and Movies." *The Libertarian Forum* 16, no. 1 (February 1982).

"Are We Being Beastly to the Gipper? Part II," "This is the Movement You Have Chosen," "Exit Marty Anderson," "Movement Jobs," "Arts and Movies," "Errata." *The Libertarian Forum* 16, no. 2 (March 1982).

"Do Deficits Matter?" *Reason* (March 1982): 45.

"To the Gold Commission," "This is the Movement You Have Chosen," "Are We Being Beastly to the Gipper? Part III." *The Libertarian Forum* 16, no. 3 (April 1982).

Review of *FDR, 1882–1945: A Centenary Remembrance*, by Joseph Alsop. "The Roosevelt Myth." *Inquiry* (April 12, 1982): 30–31.

"Oh, Oh, Oh, What a Lovely War!" "The Historical Claims to the Falklands," "Felix Morley, RIP," "Are We Being Beastly to the Gipper? Part IV," "Changing Judgments and Alliances," "Errata," "Real World Notes." *The Libertarian Forum* 16, no. 4 (May 1982).

"More on the Falklands," "Fuhrig for Senate," "Arts and Movies," "Voluntaryists Organize," "Errata." *The Libertarian Forum* 16, no. 5 (June 1982).

"Yankee Stay Home!" *Reason* (June 1982): 61.

"Double Victory for Aggression," "Flat-Rate: The Latest Con," "Houston: The Turning of the Tide," "Are We Being Beastly to the Gipper? Part V." *The Libertarian Forum* 16, no. 6 (July 1982).

"Where the Left Goes Wrong On Foreign Policy." *Inquiry* (July 1982): 29–33.

"Crane's Grand Design for Update," "The Assault on Abortion Freedom," "Don't Cry for Iraq." *The Libertarian Forum* 16, no. 6 (August 1982).

"The Flat Rate Trap." *Libertarian Vanguard* (August 1982): 12.

"Blockbuster at Billings," "The Death of Reaganomics." *The Libertarian Forum* 16, no. 7 (September 1982).

"Flat-Rate Debate." *Reason* (September 1982): 47.

"The Massacre," "Debate on ERA." *The Libertarian Forum* 16, no. 8 (October 1982).

"The Election," "The LP and the Elections," "The War in the British Movement," "New Grass-Roots Hard Money Group," "Murray! Read the Banned Issue!" "The New Libertarian Vanguard," "The Real World," "Arts and Movies," "Falkland Followup." *The Libertarian Forum* 16, no. 9 (November-December 1982).

"Any Way You Slice It." *Reason* (December 1982): 60.

"Why Leninism Is Wrong." *Libertarian Vanguard* (December 1982): 11–12, 16.

1983

BOOKS:

The Mystery of Banking. New York: Richardson and Snyder, 1983. Translated into Polish in 2005.

OTHER:

Review of *Big Business and Presidential Power*, by Kim McQuaid. "The Grand Alliance." *Inquiry* (January 1983): 40–41.

"The Economy–The Year Ahead," "Movement Memories." *The Libertarian Forum* 17, no. 1 (January 1983).

"On Coalitions and Alignments." *Common Sense* (January-February 1983): 7, 10.

"The Unemployment Crisis." *Libertarian Party News*, January-February 1983, pp. 3, 13.

"For President–Gene Burns," "The Crane Machine Revealed," "Eubie Blake: RIP," "Economic Notes," "Recommended Reading: Monopoly and Anti-Trust," "Margaret Mead: Justice At Last!" "Four Ways to Insure a 'Very' Short Phone Conversation." *The Libertarian Forum* (February 1983).

"The Judcomm Ploy." *Libertarian Vanguard* (February 1983): 9–10.

"Economist for the Free Market, Murray N. Rothbard." *The Review of the News*, 2 February 1983, pp. 39–50.

"The New Menace of Gandhism," "The Burns Campaign," "An Open Letter to the English Movement." *The Libertarian Forum* (March 1983).

"Why We're in a Depression." *Reason* (March 1983): 45, 57.

"Is Voting Unlibertarian?" (With S.M. Olmsted.) *Libertarian Vanguard* (April 1983): 1, 4–5.

"Movement Depression," "Free Fanzi," "Arts and Movies," "Crane Machine Notes." *The Libertarian Forum* (April 1983).

"Voluntaryism and Dropout-ism." *Libertarian Vanguard* (April 1983): 3–4.

"Frontlines, RIP," "Leonard Read, RIP," "Gandhism Once More," "The 'Real' Conventioneers' Guide to New York City." *The Libertarian Forum* 17, nos. 5–6 (May-June 1983).

"Abolish the Income Tax!" *Libertarian Vanguard* (June 1983): 3.

"The Editor Replies." *The Libertarian Forum* 17, nos. 7–8 (July-August 1983).

"The Evers-Rothbard Plank." *The Familist* (July-August 1983): 2.

"Rothbard on Rand." Correspondence to *Reason* (August 1983): 10, 66.

"Should Abortion Be a Crime? The Abortion Question Once More." *Libertarian Vanguard* (August 1983): 4–5, 8.

"Coupon Caper." *Reason* (September 1983): 44.

Review of *Martin Van Buren: The Romantic Age of American Politics*, by John Niven. "Principle in Politics." *Inquiry* (September 1983): 35–37.

"Total Victory–How Sweet It Is!" "Keeping Low-Tech." *The Libertarian Forum* 17, nos. 9– 10 (September-October 1983).

"Interview 2: Rothbard." *Toward Liberty* (Toronto), October-November 1983, pp. 8–9.

"New Airline Massacre: Where's the Outrage?" "The Bergland Campaign," "Life in 1984'," "Living Liberty and All That," "Reagan War Watch." *The Libertarian Forum* 17, nos. 11–12 (November-December 1983).

"The New Menace of Gandhism," "The Burns Campaign," "An Open Letter to the English Movement." *The Libertarian Forum* (March 1983).

1984

SCHOLARLY ARTICLES & CHAPTERS IN BOOKS:

"The Federal Reserve as a Cartelization Device: The Early Years, 1913–1930." Barry Siegel, ed., *Money in Crisis*. San Francisco, Calif.: Pacific Institute for Public Policy Research, and Cambridge, Mass.: Ballinger Publishing, 1984, pp. 89–136.

"The Unemployment Crisis–A Sure Cure." Bettina B. Greaves, ed., *Employment, Unemployment, and Government Projects*. Irvington-on-Hudson, N.Y.: Foundation for Economic Education, 1984.

OTHER:

"Bergland Campaign in High Gear," "Reagan War Watch, Part II." *The Libertarian Forum* 18, nos. 1–2 (January-February 1984).

"Campaign Fever '84," "Arts and Movies," "This is the Movement You Have Chosen," "New York Politics," "Still Keeping Low-Tech," "Fifteen Years Old." *The Libertarian Forum* 18, nos. 3–4 (March-April 1984).

"Ten Great Economic Myths, Part One." *The Free Market* (April 1984): 1–4. Reprinted as "Five Great Economic Myths" in Robert White's *Duck Book*. Cocoa, Fla.: American Association of Financial Professionals, October 1984, pp. 64–65. Revised as "Eight Economic Myths" by the Ludwig von Mises Institute, 1995.

"Democrats Self-Destruct," "Erick Mack and the Anarchist Case for War," "New Crane Machine Floperoo!" "Prohibition Returns!" *The Libertarian Forum* 18, nos. 5–6 (May-June 1984).

"Ten Great Economic Myths, Part Two." *The Free Market* (June 1984): 6–8.

"Patriotic Schlock: The Endless Summer," "Life in '1984'," "Democrat Convention Notes," "Arts and Movies," "The Miss America Caper," "Campaign Notes." *The Libertarian Forum* 18, nos. 7–8 (July-August 1984).

"Kondratieff Cycle: Real Or Fabricated?—Part I." *Investment Insights*, August 1984, pp. 5–7.

"Wall Street, Banks, and American Foreign Policy." *World Market Perspective*, August 1984. Reprinted by Center for Libertarian Studies, 1995.

"Theory and History." *Austrian Economics Newsletter* (Fall, 1984): 1–3.

"Creative Economic Semantics." *The Free Market* (September 1984): 3–4.

"The Kondratieff Cycle: Real Or Fabricated?—Part Two." *Investment Insights*, September 1984, pp. 2–7.

"The State of the Movement: The Implosion," "Why the Apotheosis of Ronnie?" *The Libertarian Forum* 18, nos. 8–12 (September-December 1984).

"A Walk On the Supply Side." *The Free Market* (October 1984): 3–4.

"Inflation or Deflation–Which Way?" *Johannesburg Gold & Metal Mining Advisor*, October 1984, pp. 7–8.

"Resurging Inflation Or Sudden Deflation?" *Jerome Smith's Investment Perspectives*, November 1984, pp. 1–6, 8.

Review of *Liberty Reclaimed: A New Look at American Politics*, by Jim Lewis. *Libertarian Party News*, August 1984, p. 26. Reprinted in *The Natural Law Familist* (December 1984): 2–3.

1985

SCHOLARLY ARTICLES & CHAPTERS IN BOOKS:

"Professor Hébert on Entrepreneurship." *Journal of Libertarian Studies* 7, no. 2 (Fall, 1985): 281–86. Reprinted as "Professor Kirzner on Entrepreneurship" in *The Logic of Action Two: Applications and Criticism from the Austrian School*. Cheltenham,

U.K.: Edward Elgar, 1997, pp. 245–53. Reprinted and expanded as *Economic Controversies*. Auburn, Ala.: Ludwig von Mises Institute, 2007.

"The Case for a Genuine Gold Dollar." Llewellyn H. Rockwell, Jr., *The Gold Standard: An Austrian Perspective*. Lexington, Mass.: D.C. Heath, 1985, pp. 1–17. Reprinted in *The Logic of Action One: Method, Money, and the Austrian School*. Cheltenham, U.K.: Edward Elgar, 1997, pp. 364–83. Reprinted and expanded as *Economic Controversies*. Auburn, Ala.: Ludwig von Mises Institute, 2007.

OTHER:

"Enemy of the State." Interview with Rothbard by J.W. Harris. *Chic*, sometime after 1985.

"Bringing Down the Dollar." *Issues in Economic Policy*. Auburn, Ala.: Ludwig von Mises Institute, 1985, pp. 1–2.

Introduction to *Theory and History*, by Ludwig von Mises. Auburn, Ala.: Ludwig von Mises Institute, 1985, pp. xi–xvi.

"The Flat Tax: A Skeptical View." *Issues in Economic Policy*. Auburn, Ala.: Ludwig von Mises Institute, 1985, pp. 1–14.

"Airport Congestion: A Case of Market Failure?" *The Free Market* (January 1985): 5–4.

"Competition at Work: Xerox at 25." *The Free Market* (February 1985): 1, 4.

Interview with Rothbard. *Predictions*, April 1985, pp. 5–8.

"The Politics of Famine." *The Free Market* (April 1985): 5.

"Lo, the Poor Farmer." *New York Times*, 22 May 1985.

"Flat Tax . . . or Flat Taxpayer?" *The Free Market* (June 1985): 1, 3.

"Murray Rothbard Examines Economic Mythology." *The Review of the News*, 19 June 1985, pp. 31–40. Appeared originally in two issues of *The Free Market*, April 1984 and June 1984.

"The Crusade Against South Africa." *The Free Market* (July 1985): 1, 4.

"Bankruns and Water Shortages." *The Free Market* (September 1985): 3–4.

"Deductibility and Subsidy." *The Free Market* (November 1985): 4.

"The Myth of Tax 'Reform'." *World Market Perspective* 18, no. 11 (November 1985). Reprinted in *The Logic of Action Two: Applications and Criticism from the Austrian School*. Cheltenham, U.K.: Edward Elgar, 1997, pp. 109–20. Reprinted and expanded as *Economic Controversies*. Auburn, Ala.: Ludwig von Mises Institute, 2007.

1986

OTHER:

"The Brilliance of Turgot." Auburn Ala.: The Ludwig von Mises Institute, 1986. Translated in French as "L'eclat de Turgot" by François Guillaumat in *Les Journal des Economistes et des Etudes Humaines* 6, no. 1 (March 1995): 21–42.

"The World Currency in Crisis." *The Free Market* (February 1986): 1, 3–4.

"Jim Cook Interviews Murray Rothbard." *International Gold & Silver Forecaster*, February 1986, pp. 1–5.

"Privatization." *The Free Market* (March 1986): 3–4.

Review of *Money and Freedom*, by Hans Sennholz. "Another Round in the Gold Debate." *Reason* (April 1986): 50, 52.

"Why Should Texaco be Liable?" *Individual Liberty*. Warminster, Penn.: Society for Individual Liberty, May 1986, p. 8.

"A Trip to Poland." *The Free Market* (June 1986): 1, 4.

"Murray N. Rothbard on Hermeneutics." *Austrian Economics Newsletter* (Fall, 1986): 12.

"Money Inflation and Price Inflation." *The Free Market* (September 1986): 1, 3.

"First Step Back to Gold." *The Free Market* (November 1986): 1–3.

"Government vs. Natural Resources." *The Free Market* (December 1986): 1, 5.

1987

SCHOLARLY ARTICLES & CHAPTERS IN BOOKS:

"Breaking Out of the Walrasian Box: The Cases of Schumpeter and Hansen." *Review of Austrian Economics* 1 (1987): 97–108. Reprinted in *The Logic of Action Two: Applications and Criticism from the Austrian School*. Cheltenham, U.K.: Edward Elgar, 1997, pp. 226–40. Reprinted and expanded as *Economic Controversies*. Auburn, Ala.: Ludwig von Mises Institute, 2007.

"Catallactics." *The New Palgrave: A Dictionary of Economics*, vol. 1, by John Eatwell, Murray Milgate, and Peter Newman, eds. New York: The Stockton Press, 1987, pp. 377–78.

"Fetter, Frank Albert (1863–1949)." *The New Palgrave: A Dictionary of Economics*, vol. 2, by John Eatwell, Murray Milgate, and Peter Newman, eds. New York: The Stockton Press, 1987, p. 308.

"Imputation." *The New Palgrave: A Dictionary of Economics*, vol. 2, by John Eatwell, Murray Milgate, and Peter Newman, eds. New York: The Stockton Press, 1987, pp. 738–39.

"Introductory Editorial" (with Walter Block). *Review of Austrian Economics* 1 (1987): ix–xiii.

"Mises, Ludwig Edler von (1881–1973)." *The New Palgrave: A Dictionary of Economics*, vol. 1, by John Eatwell, Murray Milgate, and Peter Newman, eds. New York: The Stockton Press, 1987, pp. 479–80.

"Time Preference." *The New Palgrave: A Dictionary of Economics*, vol. 4, by John Eatwell, Murray Milgate, and Peter Newman, eds. New York: The Stockton Press, 1987, pp. 644–46. Reprinted in *Capital Theory*, by John Eatwell, Murray Milgate, and Peter Newman, eds. New York: W.W. Norton, 1990. Reprinted in *Austrian Economics: A Reader* by Richard M. Ebeling, ed. Hillsdale, Mich.: Hillsdale College Press, 1991, pp. 414–22.

OTHER:

Review of *The Passion of Ayn Rand*, by Barbara Branden. *American Libertarian*, sometime between 1987 and 1989.

"The Sociology of the Ayn Rand Cult." Port Townsend, Wash.: Liberty Publishing, 1987.

"The Homeless and the Hungry and the . . ." *The Free Market* (February 1987): 1, 5.

"Freedom is for Everyone (Including the despised 'Rightists')." *Liberty* (March 1987): 43–44.

"Me and the Eiger." *Liberty* (March 1987): 60.

"Gold Socialism or Dollar Socialism?" *The Free Market* (April 1987): 1–2.

"The Consequences of Human Action: Intended or Unintended?" *The Free Market* (May 1987): 3–4.

"For President: Ron Paul." *American Libertarian* (June 1987): 1–3.

"Panic on Wall Street." *The Free Market* (June 1987): 3, 7.

"Alan Greenspan: A Minority Report on the New Fed Chairman." *The Free Market* (August 1987): 3, 8.

"Life or Death in Seattle." *Liberty* (August 1987): 39–42.

"Adam Smith Reconsidered." *Austrian Economics Newsletter* (Fall, 1987): 5–7. Reprinted in *Austrian Economics*, vol. 1, by Stephen Littlechild. Brookfield, Vt.: Edward Elgar, 1990, pp. 41–44.

"Keynesian Myths." *The Free Market* (September 1987): 3–4.

Review of *Crisis and Leviathan*, by Robert Higgs. "The Rise of Statism." *Liberty* (September-October 1987): 31–32.

"The Balanced-Budget Amendment Hoax." *The Free Market* (October 1987): 3.

"The Specter of Airline Re-Regulation." *The Free Market* (November 1987): 1, 3.

"Back to Fixed Exchange Rates: Another 'New Economic Order'." *The Free Market* (December 1987): 10–12.

1988

BOOKS:

Ludwig von Mises: Scholar, Creator, Hero. Auburn, Ala.: Ludwig von Mises Institute, 1988.

SCHOLARLY ARTICLES & CHAPTERS IN BOOKS:

"The Myth of Free Banking in Scotland." *Review of Austrian Economics* 2 (1988): 229–45. Reprinted in *The Logic of Action Two: Applications and Criticism from the Austrian School.* Cheltenham, U.K.: Edward Elgar, 1997, pp. 311–30. Reprinted and expanded as *Economic Controversies.* Auburn, Ala.: Ludwig von Mises Institute, 2007.

"Timberlake on the Austrian Theory of Money: A Comment." *Review of Austrian Economics* 2 (1992): 179–87.

OTHER:

"Nine Myths About the Crash." *The Free Market* (January 1988): 1–3.

"The Interest Rate Question." *The Free Market* (February 1988): 1, 8.

"Chaos Theory: Destroying Mathematical Economics From Within?" *The Free Market* (March 1988): 1–2, 8.

"Babbitry and Taxes: A Profile in Courage?" *The Free Market* (April 1988): 3.

"The Story of the Mises Institute." *The Free Market* (May 1988): 1–2, 8.

"The National Bureau and Business Cycles." *The Free Market* (June 1988): 3, 5.

"Dancing with Joy in Saigon and Washington." *Liberty* (July 1988): 11–12.

"Silly Out of Season." *Liberty* (July 1988): 11.

"The Libertarian Family and Entrepreneurship." *Liberty* (July 1988): 9–10.

"The Political Circus." *Liberty* (July 1988): 13.

"The Return of the Tax Credit." *The Free Market* (July 1988): 1, 3.

"William Harold Hutt, in Memoriam." *The Free Market* (September 1988): 4–5.

"The Collapse of Socialism." *The Free Market* (October 1988): 3.

"Beyond Is And Ought." *Liberty* (November 1988): 44–45.

"That Cato Seminar." *Liberty* (November 1988): 7–8.

"The Next Four Years." *The Free Market* (November 1988): 1–3.

"The Tall and the Short of Genocide." *Liberty* (November 1988): 6.

"Outlawing Jobs: The Minimum Wage, Once More." *The Free Market* (December 1988): 1, 7–8.

1989

SCHOLARLY ARTICLES & CHAPTERS IN BOOKS:

"The Hermeneutical Invasion of Philosophy and Ethics." *Review of Austrian Economics* 3 (1989): 45–59. Reprinted in *The Logic of Action Two: Applications and Criticism from the Austrian School.* Cheltenham, U.K.: Edward Elgar, 1997, pp. 275–93. Reprinted and expanded as *Economic Controversies.* Auburn, Ala.: Ludwig von Mises Institute, 2007.

"World War I as Fulfillment: Power and the Intellectuals." *Journal of Libertarian Studies* 9, no. 1 (Winter, 1989): 81–125. Reprinted in *The Costs of War: America's Pyrrhic Victories*, by John V. Denson, ed. New Brunswick, N.J.: Transaction Publishers, 1997. Second expanded edition, 1999, pp. 249–99.

OTHER:

"The Other Side of the Coin: Free Banking in Chile." *Austrian Economics Newsletter* (Winter, 1989): 1–4.

"Keynesianism Redux." *The Free Market* (January 1989): 1, 3–5.

"Greenhouse Effects." *Liberty* (January 1989): 13–14.

"Statistics: Destroyed from Within?" *The Free Market* (February 1989): 3.

"Chester Alan Arthur and the 1988 Campaign." *Liberty* (March 1989): 11, 22.

"Ronald Reagan: An Autopsy." *Liberty* (March 1989): 13–22.

"Q&A on the S&L Mess." *The Free Market* (April 1989): 1–3.

"Inflation Redux." *The Free Market* (May 1989): 1, 3–4.

"Eyeing the Top of the Pyramid." *Liberty* (May 1989): 13–15.

"Public Choice: A Misshapen Tool." *Liberty* (May 1989): 20 21.

"Michael R. Milken vs. the Power Elite." *The Free Market* (June 1989): 1, 7–8.

"The Keynesian Dream." *The Free Market* (July 1989): 2.

"Why Not Feel Sorry for Exxon?" *Liberty* (July 1989): 7–8.

"Kiss and Tell." Review of *Judgment Day*, by Nathaniel Branden. *American Libertarian* (August 1989): 2, 5–6.

"The Freedom of Revolution." *The Free Market* (August 1989): 1, 8.

"Her Feet's Too Big!" *Liberty* (September 1989): 7.

"How To Desocialize?" *The Free Market* (September 1989): 1, 3.

"My Break With Branden and the Rand Cult." *Liberty* (September 1989): 27–32.

"The Revenge of the Luftmenschen." *American Libertarian* (September 1989): 1, 6–7.

"Ludwig von Mises's Neglected Classic." *The Free Market* (October 1989): 4.

"Are Savings Too Low?" *The Free Market* (November 1989): 7–8.

"Loathing the Fear in New York." *Liberty* (November 1989): 29–32.

"Two Cheers for Webster." *Liberty* (November 1989): 7.

"Government and Hurricane Hugo: A Deadly Combination." *The Free Market* (December 1989): 1, 4, 8.

1990

SCHOLARLY ARTICLES & CHAPTERS IN BOOKS:

"Time Preference." John Eatwell, Murray Milgate, and Peter Newman, eds., *Capital Theory*. New York: W.W. Norton, 1990. Reprinted in *Austrian Economics: A Reader* by Richard M. Ebeling, ed. Hillsdale, Mich.: Hillsdale College Press, 1991, pp. 414–22.

"Karl Marx: Communist as Religious Eschatologist." *Review of Austrian Economics*, 4 (1990): 123–79. Reprinted in *The Logic of Action Two: Applications and Criticism from the Austrian School*. Cheltenham, U.K.: Edward Elgar, 1997, pp. 331–99. Reprinted and expanded as *Economic Controversies*. Auburn, Ala.: Ludwig von Mises Institute, 2007.

"Concepts of the Role of Intellectuals In Social Change Toward Laissez Faire." *Journal of Libertarian Studies* 9, no. 2 (Fall, 1990): 43–67.

OTHER:

"A Gold Standard for Russia?" *The Free Market* (January 1990): 3.

"Kingdom Come: The Politics of the Millennium." *Liberty* (January 1990): 9–42, 45.

"Welcoming the Vietnamese." *The Free Market* (February 1990): 3.

"Hoppephobia." *Liberty* (March 1990): 11–12.

"A Radical Prescription for the Socialist Bloc." *The Free Market* (March 1990): 1, 3–4.

"That Infamous Diary." *Chronicles* (April 1990): 31–33.

"The Social Security Swindle." *The Free Market* (April 1990): 1, 3.

"Why The Report?" "Farewell Speeches to the Alabama LP," "Arts and Movies," "The Post-Cold War World." *Rothbard-Rockwell Report* 1, no. 1 (April 1990).

"Foreign Policy for the Post-Cold War World." *Chronicles* (May 1990): 16–20.

"Inflation and the Spin Doctors." *The Free Market* (May 1990): 5–6.

"Why Paleo?" "Postrel and 'Dynanism'," "The Real Lesson of Ryan White." *Rothbard-Rockwell Report* 1, no. 1 (May 1990).

"Mrs. Thatcher's Poll Tax." *The Free Market* (June 1990): 1, 3.

"Peru: What Happened on the Way to The Free Market." *The Free Market* (July 1990): 1, 3.

"The Women/Ladies/Girls/Spoiled Brats of Mills," "Guilt Sanctified," "LP Self-Destruction: The Lear Scandal," "Arts and Movies." *Rothbard-Rockwell Report* 1, no. 3 (July 1990).

"The Economics of Government 'Medical Insurance'." *The Free Market* (August 1990): 1, 6–7.

"The Nationalities Question," "Our Pro-Death Culture," "The Flag Flap." *Rothbard-Rockwell Report* 1, no. 4 (August 1990).

"Letter From New York City: It Was a Long, Hot Summer." *Chronicles* (September 1990): 42–44.

"Mr. Rothbard Replies." *Chronicles* (September 1990): 5–6.

"The Life and Death of the Old Right," "'Free Market' Environmentalists." *Rothbard-Rockwell Report* 1, no. 5 (September 1990).

"The 'Partnership' of Government and Business." *Free Market* (September 1990): 1, 3–4.

"Mr. Bush's War." *Rothbard-Rockwell Report* 1 no. 6 (October 1990).

"Oil Prices Again." *The Free Market* (October 1990): 1, 3–4.

"Purity and Libertarian Politics," "I Hate Max Lerner," "Down With the D-e-e-fense," "Sports, Politics, and the Constitution," "Arts and Movies." *Rothbard-Rockwell Report* 1, no. 7 (November 1990).

"Why the Intervention in Arabia?" *The Free Market* (November 1990): 1, 3–4.

"Affirmative Scholarship." *Chronicles* (December 1990): 32–34.

"Pat Buchanan and the Menace of Anti-Anti-Semitism," "Stuck in the Sixties," "Arts and Movies." *Rothbard-Rockwell Report* 1, no. 8 (December 1990).

"The Budget 'Crisis'." *The Free Market* (December 1990): 1, 4–5.

1991

BOOKS:

The Case for a 100 Percent Gold Dollar. Auburn, Ala.: Ludwig von Mises Institute, 1991.

Freedom, Inequality, Primitivism, and the Division of Labor. Auburn, Ala.: Ludwig von Mises Institute, 1991.

SCHOLARLY ARTICLES & CHAPTERS IN BOOKS:

"The End of Socialism and the Calculation Debate Revisited." *Review of Austrian Economics* 5, no. 2 (1991): 51–76. Reprinted in *The Logic of Action One: Method, Money, and the Austrian School*. Cheltenham, U.K.: Edward Elgar, 1997, pp. 408–37. Reprinted and expanded as *Economic Controversies*. Auburn, Ala.: Ludwig von Mises Institute, 2007.

"Introduction to the French Edition of *Ethics of Liberty*." *Journal of Libertarian Studies* 10, no. 1 (Fall, 1991): 11–22.

OTHER:

"Inflationary Recession, Once More." *The Free Market* (January 1991): 1, 5.

"The 'New Fusionism': A Movement For Our Time," "On Being Negative," "The Case for 'Hypocrisy'," "Election Oddities," "The Kulturkampf Corner." *Rothbard-Rockwell Report* 2, no. 1 (January 1991).

"Exit the Iron Lady." *The Free Market* (February 1991): 6–7.

"Mr. Bush's Shooting War," "'Date Rape' on Campus." *Rothbard-Rockwell Report* 2, no. 2 (February 1991).

"Bank Crisis!" *The Free Market* (March 1991): 1–3.

"Notes on the Nintendo War," "Bruno Bettelheim; Plagiarist, Sadist, Child Abuser," "Combatting 'Hate Speech'." *Rothbard-Rockwell Report* 2, no. 3 (March 1991).

"Deflation, Free or Compulsory." *The Free Market* (April 1991): 1, 3–4.

"The Insensitivity Squad." *Chronicles* (April 1991): 7–8.

"The Menace of Egalitarianism," "Lessons of the Gulf War," "George Herbert Walker Bush: The Power and the Glory." *Rothbard-Rockwell Report* 2, no. 4 (April 1991).

"Conservative Movement: R.I.P.?" *Chronicles* (May 1991): 20–21.

"The Glorious Postwar World." *The Free Market* (May 1991): 5.

"Why the War? The Kuwait Connection," "Education: Rethinking 'Choice'," "Diversity, Death, and Reason." *Rothbard-Rockwell Report* 2, no. 5 (May 991).

"The Infant Mortality Crisis." *The Free Market* (June 1991): 1, 3–4.

"We Make the Big Time!" "The Kennedy 'Rape' Case," "The Kennedy Case: What Kind of Republican?" "Yugoslavian Breakup," "The Deaf and the Blind." *Rothbard-Rockwell Report* 2, no. 6 (June 1991).

"Lessons of the Recession." *The Free Market* (July 1991): 4–5.

"The Right to Kill, With Dignity?" "Rockwell vs. Rodney and the Libertarian World," "The Road to Rome?" "Contra Don Feder." *Rothbard-Rockwell Report* 2, no. 7 (July 1991).

"Marshall, Civil Rights, and the Court," "Exhume! Exhume! Or, Who Put the Arsenic in Rough-n-Ready's Cherries?" "Is God A Man?" "Degrees of Punishment," "Nobel for Buckley?" *Rothbard-Rockwell Report* 2, no. 8 (August 1991).

"Should We Bail Out Gorby?" *The Free Market* (August 1991): 1, 4–5.

"Letter From Academia." *Chronicles* (September 1991): 48–49.

"Undercounting Hispanics," "Judge Thomas and Black Nationalism," "'Tolerance,' Or Manners?" "Welcome, Slovenia!" *Rothbard-Rockwell Report* 2, no. 9 (September 1991).

"What To Do Until Privatization Comes." *The Free Market* (September 1991): 1, 8.

"Education and the Jeffries Flap," "Wichita Justice? On Denationalizing the Courts," "Who Dissed Whom? Or, Do Africans Hate Blacks?" "Requiem for Dick Bodie." *Rothbard-Rockwell Report* 2, no. 10 (October 1991).

"Letter From New York: The Long Hot Summer." *Chronicles* (October 1991): 45–46.

"The Mysterious Fed." *The Free Market* (October 1991): 1, 7.

"Lessons of the Three Days in August," "Cry for Christian Science," "The Cyprus Question," "Ron Paul for President" (with Llewellyn H. Rockwell, Jr.). *Rothbard-Rockwell Report* 2, no. 11 (November 1991).

"The Salomon Brothers Scandal." *The Free Market* (November 1991): 1, 7.

"The Great Thomas & Hill Show: Stopping the Monstrous Regiment," "Tips for Wannabees," "Mr. First Nighter." *Rothbard-Rockwell Report* 2, no. 12 (December 1991).

"The Union Problem." *The Free Market* (December 1991): 1, 6–7.

1992

SCHOLARLY ARTICLES & CHAPTERS IN BOOKS:

Review of *Gold, Greenbacks, and the Constitution*, by Richard H. Timberlake. "Aurophobia, or, Free Banking on What Standard?" *Review of Austrian Economics* 6, no. 1 (1992): 65–77.

"How and How Not To Desocialize." *Review of Austrian Economics* 6, no. 1 (1992): 65–77. Reprinted in *The Logic of Action Two: Applications and Criticism from the Austrian School*. Cheltenham, U.K.: Edward Elgar, 1997, pp. 200–13. Reprinted and expanded as *Economic Controversies*. Auburn, Ala.: Ludwig von Mises Institute, 2007.

"Keynes, the Man." Mark Skousen, ed., *Dissent on Keynes: A Critical Appraisal of Keynesian Economics*. New York: Praeger Publishers, 1992, pp. 171–98.

"The Present State of Austrian Economics." Working Paper from the Ludwig von Mises Institute, November 1992. Reprinted in *The Logic of Action One: Method, Money, and the Austrian School.* Cheltenham, U.K.: Edward Elgar, 1997, pp. 111–72. Reprinted in *Journal des Economistes et des Etudes Humaines* 6, no. 1 (March 1995): 43–89. Reprinted and expanded as *Economic Controversies.* Auburn, Ala.: Ludwig von Mises Institute, 2007.

OTHER:

"Clinton och media." Interview with Rothbard. *Svensk Linje*, nr. 4–6, 1992, pp. 38–39.

"I stället för EMS och ECU." Interview with Rothbard. *Svensk Linje*, nr. 4–6, 1992, pp. 40–42.

"For President: Pat Buchanan," "Buchanan for President" (with Llewellyn H. Rockwell, Jr.), "Right-Wing Populism," "Time for War!" *Rothbard-Rockwell Report* 3, no. 1 (January 1992).

"The Recession Explained." *The Free Market* (January 1992): 1, 7–8.

"Buchanan an Anti-Semite ? It's a Smear." *Los Angeles Times*, 6 January 1992, p. 7.

"Feeble Nibbles at the Edges of Tax Reform." *Los Angeles Times*, 30 January 1992, p. B7.

"Bush and the Recession." *The Free Market* (February 1992): 1, 6–7.

"Pat Buchanan and His Critics," "Pat Buchanan and the Old Right," "New World Order, Haiti Department," "The Smith 'Rape' Case." *Rothbard-Rockwell Report* 3, no. 2 (February 1992).

"Listening to the Ayes of Taxes." *The Washington Times*, 8 February 1992.

"A Strategy for the Right." Speech delivered before the John Randolph Club, January 1992. Reprinted in *Rothbard-Rockwell Report* 3, no. 3 (March 1992). Excerpts reprinted in *National Review* (March 16, 1992): S28–32.

"'Free Trade' in Perspective." *The Free Market* (March 1992): 1, 7.

"His Only Crime Was Against the Old Guard." *Los Angeles Times*, 3 March 1992, B7.

"Are We Under-Taxed?" *The Free Market* (April 1992): 5, 8.

"Letter from Murray N. Rothbard," "Max Lerner: Again?!" *Rothbard-Rockwell Report* 3, no. 4 (April 1992).

"Letter From New York: Long Hot Summer, Long Cold Winter." *Chronicles* (April 1992): 42– 45.

"Anti-Buchanania: A Mini-Encyclopedia," "The J.F.K. Flap." *Rothbard-Rockwell Report* 3, no. 5 (May 1992).

"Coping With Street Crime." *Chronicles* (May 1992): 47–49.

"Rethinking the '80s." *The Free Market* (May 1992): 1, 8.

"Friedrich August von Hayek, 1899–1992." *The Free Market* (June 1992): 4–5.

"Repudiating the National Debt." *Chronicles* (June 1992): 49–52.

"The Evil Empire Strikes Back: The Neocons and Us," "Ex-Yugoslavia," "Perot & The Populist Upsurge." *Rothbard-Rockwell Report* 3, no. 6 (June 1992).

"Perot and Perotphobia," "Anarchists in Poland," "Mr. First Nighter." *Rothbard-Rockwell Report* 3, no. 7 (July 1992).

"Rioting for Rage, Fun, and Profit." *The Free Market* (July 1992): 3, 5.

"After Perot, What?" "Roy Childs, Hail and Farewell!" *Rothbard-Rockwell Report* 3, no. 8 (August 1992).

"Perot, the Constitution, and Direct Democracy." *The Free Market* (August 1992): 4–5.

"The Neocon Welfare State." *The Free Market* (September 1992): 1, 7.

"Working Our Way Back to the President," "Reply to Raimondo: Whom to Root For in November," "Gang-Stabbing the President: What, Who, and Why," "Ex-Czechoslovakia," "U.S., Keep Out of Bosnia!" *Rothbard-Rockwell Report* 3, no. 9 (September 1992).

"By Their Fruits . . ." *The Free Market* (October 1992): 4–5.

"Kulturkampf!" "Bobby Fischer: The Lynching of the Returning Hero," "Liberal Hysteria: The Mystery Explained." *Rothbard-Rockwell Report* 3, no. 10 (October 1992).

"Are Diamonds Really Forever?" *The Free Market* (November 1992): 5–6.

"Up from the Libertarian Party: the Houston Convention," "*The New York Times*, Communism, and South Africa." *Rothbard-Rockwell Report* 3, no. 11 (November 1992).

"Discussing the 'Issues'." *The Free Market* (December 1992): 3–4.

"Fluoridation Revisited." *The New American*, 14 December 1992, pp. 36–39.

"Stealing." *Chronicles* (December 1992).

"Hold Back the Hordes for 4 More Years." *Los Angeles Times*, 30 July 1992, A11–12.

"America, Keep Out of Bosnia: People in Plush Offices are Thirsting for Blood, Which Our Youth Will have to Supply. Why?" *Los Angeles Times*, 13 August 1992, A11–12.

1993

SCHOLARLY ARTICLES & CHAPTERS IN BOOKS:

"Mises and the Role of the Economist in Public Policy." Jeffrey M. Herbener, ed., *The Meaning of Ludwig von Mises*. Norwell, Mass.: Kluwer Academic Publishers, 1993, pp. 193–208.

OTHER:

"The Clinton Economic Plan." Report published by the Ludwig von Mises Institute, 1993.

"Clintonomics: The Prospect." *The Free Market* (January 1993): 1, 3–4.

"Letter From New York: The Saga of Esteban Solarz." *Chronicles* (January 1993): 41–42.

"The 'Watershed' Election," "Fiscally Conservative, Socially Tolerant," "Fluoridation Revisited." *Rothbard-Rockwell Report* 4, no. 1 (January 1993).

"'Fairness' and the Steel Steal." *The Free Market* (February 1993): 1, 6–7.

"Human Rights Are Property Rights." *The Classical Liberal*. Boise, Idaho: Center for the Study of Market Alternatives, February 1993, pp. 5–7.

"Letter From New York: The Year of the Italian Nonwoman." *Chronicles* (February 1993): 44–46.

"The Religious Right: Toward A Coalition," "Ethnic Fury In The Caucuses: Sorting It Out," "Their Malcolm . . . And Mine," "The December Surprise," "Mr. First Nighter." *Rothbard-Rockwell Report* 4, no. 2 (February 1993).

"Book Reviews." *Austrian Economics Newsletter* (Spring, 1993): 13–14.

"In Search of Al Gore's Heckscher," "But What About The Hungarians?" "Coping With the Inaugural," "'Doing God's Work' in Somalia'," "John Silber: Doing Well Doing Neocon Good." *Rothbard-Rockwell Report* 4, no. 3 (March 1993).

"That Gasoline Tax." *The Free Market* (March 1993): 1, 5–6.

"Environmentalists Clobber Texas." *The Free Market* (April 1993): 3–4.

"Phony Libertarians and the War for the Republican Soul," "Free Speech, 1, Hate Thought Police, 1." *Rothbard-Rockwell Report* 4, no. 4 (April 1993).

"Clintonomics Revealed." *The Free Market* (May 1993): 1, 7–8.

"Great Book 'Suppressed'!" "Self-Therapy and the Clintonian State," "The Oscars," "A French Masterpiece!" *Rothbard-Rockwell Report* 4, no. 5 (May 1993).

"Hands Off the Serbs!" "'Debauchery! Debauchery!' At Tailhook," "The Bosnian Serbs Stand Tall," "Kaza's First Hundred Days," "On 'Taking Responsibility' for Waco," "On The King Beating TriAla.: A Note." *Rothbard-Rockwell Report* 4, no. 6 (June 1993).

"Price Controls Are Back!" *The Free Market* (June 1993): 1, 7–8.

"The Two Faces of Billary," "Anti-War Alliance Lives!" "The Arkansas-Stephens Connection," "Warning! On Bret Schundler." *Rothbard-Rockwell Report* 4, no. 7 (July 1993).

"The Legacy of Cesar Chavez." *The Free Market* (July-August 1993): 1, 5–6.

"V. Orval Watts, 1898–1993." *The Free Market* (July-August 1993): 8.

"Who Are the 'Terrorists'?" "New York Politics '93," "Goldwater Reconsidered," "How to Become a Happy Martyr." *Rothbard-Rockwell Report* 4, no. 8 (August 1993).

"When Currencies Are 'Attacked'." *The Journal of Commerce* (August 12, 1993).

"Margit von Mises, 1890–1993." *The Free Market* (September 1993): 1, 7.

"On Resisting Evil," "Is Clinton a Bastard?" "Where Intervene Next?" "Fostergate!" "Losing The Culture War: Republicans Roll Over For The Left." *Rothbard-Rockwell Report* 4, no. 9 (September 1993).

"The Clinton Health Plan: The Devil's in the Principles." *Essays in Political Economy* no. 17. Auburn, Ala.: Ludwig von Mises Institute, 1993.

"The Israel-P.L.O. Accord," "Stop Nafta," "Anti-Anti-Semitism Gone Bananas." *Rothbard-Rockwell Report* 4, no. 10 (October 1993).

"The Nafta Myth." *The Free Market* (October 1993): 1, 7–8.

"Attacking the Franc." *The Free Market* (November 1993): 4, 8.

"Why the Pro-Nafta Hysteria?" "The Bringing Down of Liz Holtzman," "Heil Yeltsin?" "Behind Waco." *Rothbard-Rockwell Report* 4, no. 11 (November 1993).

"The Big Government Libertarians: The Anti-Left-Libertarian Manifesto," "The Anti-Clinton Election," "Bosnian Update: No Peace, No Peace-Keeping." *Rothbard-Rockwell Report* 4, no. 12 (December 1993).

"The Health Plan's Devilish Principles." *The Free Market* (December 1993): 1, 7–8.

"What's the Cache of a Tax on Gas?" *The Washington Times*, 2 February 1993, Section G.

1994

BOOKS:

The Case Against the Fed. Auburn, Ala.: Ludwig von Mises Institute, 1994. Translated into Japanese in 2003.

SCHOLARLY ARTICLES & CHAPTERS IN BOOKS:

"The Consumption Tax: A Critique." *Review of Austrian Economics* 7, no. 2 (1994): 75–90.

"Nations by Consent: Decomposing the Nation-State." *Journal of Libertarian Studies* 11, no. 1 (Fall, 1994): 1–10.

OTHER:

"Eisnerize America." *Southern Heritage* 2, no. 5 (1994): 7–8.

"The Lessons of the Nafta Struggle: What Next?" "The Brady Bunch," "The Halperin Case," "Korean War Redux?" "Health Insurance: The Clintons' Phony Populism." *Rothbard-Rockwell Report* 5, no. 1 (January 1994).

"Vouchers: What Went Wrong?" *The Free Market* (January 1994): 1, 8.

"Is There Life After Nafta?" *The Free Market* (February 1994): 4, 8.

"Zhirinovsky: Yet Another 'Hitler'?" "The Virginia Senate Race: North vs. Miller," "Kristol On Buchanan: What Goes On Here?" "Impeach Boo-Boo!" "Mary Cummins Vindicated!" *Rothbard-Rockwell Report* 5, no. 2 (February 1994).

"Who Killed Vince Foster?" "More On Who Killed Vince Foster?" "Within a Month! The Bringing Down of Bobby Ray Inman," "First Fruits of Nafta: The Mexican Revolution," "Vatican-Israel Rapprochement," "Arts and Movies." *Rothbard-Rockwell Report* 5, no. 3 (March 1994).

"The Economics of Gun Control." *The Free Market* (March 1994): 4–5.

"The Vital Importance of Separation," "The Foster Body and Park Police," "Russia's Triumph at Sarajevo," "Hillary's 'Health Care': Shafting the Elderly." *Rothbard-Rockwell Report* 5, no. 4 (April 1994).

"Welfare As We Don't Know It." *The Free Market* (April 1994): 1, 8.

"Reign of Terror in Little Rock," "Clintonian Ugly," "Will Super-Gergen Save the Day?" "Those Jury Verdicts." *Rothbard-Rockwell Report* 5, no. 5 (May 1994).

"The Trouble With Quick Fixes." *The Free Market* (May 1994): 1, 8.

"Hutus vs. Tutsis," "The Apotheosis of Tricky Dick," "Howard Stern for Governor?" "American Jewry Saved!" "Rumor Unfounded." *Rothbard-Rockwell Report* 5, no. 6 (June 1994).

"Stocks, Bonds, and Rule by Fools." *The Free Market* (June 1994): 1, 7–8.

"The Case Against Fixed Currencies." *The Journal of Commerce* (June 7, 1994).

"Fixed-Rate Fictions." *The Free Market* (July 1994): 3–4.

"Revolution in Italy!" "The Franciscan Way." *Rothbard-Rockwell Report* 5, no. 7 (July 1994).

"America's Most Persecuted Minority," "Hunting the Christian Right." *Rothbard-Rockwell Report* 5, no. 8 (August 1994).

"Eisnerizing Manassas." *The Free Market* (August 1994): 1, 8.

"Life in the Old Right." *Chronicles* (August 1994): 15–19.

"Invade the World," "The New York Political Circus," "For Mel Bradford," "Rumor Unfounded." *Rothbard-Rockwell Report* 5, no. 9 (September 1994).

"The Whiskey Rebellion." *The Free Market* (September 1994): 1, 8.

"A New Strategy for Liberty," "Cuba: A Modest Proposal," "Nafta and the 'Free Trade' Hoax," "The Menace of the Religious Left," "Dead Wrong." *Rothbard-Rockwell Report* 5, no. 10 (October 1994).

"Economic Incentives and Welfare." *The Free Market* (October 1994): 7.

"Big-Government Libertarians." Speech delivered before the John Randolph Club, October 21, 1994. Reprinted in *Rothbard-Rockwell Report* 5, no. 11 (November 1994).

"Population 'Control'." *The Free Market* (November 1994): 4–5.

"Race! That Murray Book," "St. Hillary and the Religious Left," "The Paradigm Kid." *Rothbard-Rockwell Report* 5, no. 12 (December 1994).

"The War on the Car." *The Free Market* (December 1994): 4–5.

1995

BOOKS:

An Austrian Perspective on the History of Economic Thought, vol. 1: *Economic Thought Before Adam Smith*. Brookfield, Vt.: Edward Elgar, 1995. Translated in Spanish by F. Basáñez and R. Imaz as Historia del Pensamiento Económico, vol. 1: El Pensamiento Económico Hasta Adam Smith. Madrid: Unión Editorial, S.A., 1999. New printing Auburn, Ala.: Ludwig von Mises Institute, 2006.

An Austrian Perspective on the History of Economic Thought, vol. 2: *Classical Economics*. Brookfield, Vt.: Edward Elgar, 1995. New printing Auburn, Ala.: Ludwig von Mises Institute, 2006.

Wall Street, Banks, and American Foreign Policy. Burlingame, Calif: Center for Libertarian Studies, 1995. Originally appeared in *World Market Perspective,* August 1984.

Making Economic Sense. Auburn, Ala.: Ludwig von Mises Institute, 1995. Second edition published in 2006.

SCHOLARLY ARTICLES & CHAPTERS IN BOOKS:

"Bureaucracy and the Civil Service in the United States." *Journal of Libertarian Studies* 11, no. 2 (Summer, 1995): 3–75.

OTHER:

"The November Revolution and Its Betrayal," "King Kristol," "A Rivederci, Mario." *Rothbard-Rockwell Report* 6, no. 1 (January 1995).

"1996! The Morning Line," "Random Gripes." *Rothbard-Rockwell Report* 6, no. 2 (February 1995).

"The Revolution Comes Home." *The Free Market* (January 1995): 4–5.

"Fractional Reserve Banking." *The Freeman* (October 1995).

"Is It 'The Economy, Stupid'?" *The Free Market* (February 1995): 4–5.

1996

SCHOLARLY ARTICLES & CHAPTERS IN BOOKS:

"Origins of the Welfare State in America." *Journal of Libertarian Studies* 12, no. 2 (Fall, 1996): 193–229.

"Economic Depressions: Their Cause and Cure." *The Austrian Theory of the Trade Cycle and Other Essays.* Auburn, Ala.: Ludwig von Mises Institute, 1996, pp. 37–64. Originally published by the Center for Libertarian Studies, 1978.

1997

BOOKS:

The Logic of Action One: Method, Money, and the Austrian School. Cheltenham, U.K.: Edward Elgar, 1997. Reprinted and expanded as *Economic Controversies.* Auburn, Ala.: Ludwig von Mises Institute, 2007.

The Logic of Action Two: Applications and Criticism from the Austrian School. Cheltenham, U.K.: Edward Elgar, 1997. Reprinted and expanded as *Economic Controversies.* Auburn, Ala.: Ludwig von Mises Institute, 2007.

SCHOLARLY ARTICLES & CHAPTERS IN BOOKS:

"The Gold-Exchange Standard in the Interwar Years." Kevin Dowd and Richard H. Timberlake, Jr., eds., *Money and the Nation State.* Oakland, Calif.: Independent Institute, 1998, pp. 105–67.

"The Political Thought of Étienne de la Boétie." An Introduction to *The Politics of Obedience: The Discourse of Voluntary Servitude* by Étienne de la Boétie. New York: Black Rose Books, 1997, pp. 9–42.

"America's Two Just Wars: 1775 and 1861." John V. Denson, ed., *The Costs of War: America's Pyrrhic Victories*. New Brunswick, N.J.: Transaction Publishers, 1997. Second expanded edition, 1999, pp. 119–33.

"World War I as Fulfillment: Power and the Intellectuals." John V. Denson, ed., *The Costs of War: America's Pyrrhic Victories*. New Brunswick, N.J.: Transaction Publishers, 1997. Second expanded edition, 1999, pp. 249–99.

OTHER:

"Buchanan and Tullock's The Calculus of Consent." *The Logic of Action Two: Applications and Criticism from the Austrian School.* Cheltenham, U.K.: Edward Elgar, 1997, pp. 269–74. Excerpted from a letter to Dr. Ivan R. Bierly of the William Volker Fund, dated August 17, 1960. Reprinted and expanded as *Economic Controversies*. Auburn, Ala.: Ludwig von Mises Institute, 2007.

1998

SCHOLARLY ARTICLES & CHAPTERS IN BOOKS:

"America's Two Just Wars: 1775 and 1861." John V. Denson, ed. *The Costs of War: America's Pyrrhic Victories*, 2nd edition. New Brunswick, N.J.: Transactions Publishers, 1998, pp. 119–33. This chapter is composed from notes used by Rothbard in his presentation at the "Costs of War" conference, May 22, 1994, presented by the Ludwig von Mises Institute.

2000

BOOK:

Egalitarianism As a Revolt Against Nature and Other Essays. Washington, D.C.: Libertarian Review Press, 1974. See article by this title (excluding "and Other Essays") in *Modern Age* (Fall, 1973): 348–57. Reprinted Auburn, Ala.: Ludwig von Mises Institute, 2000.

2005

BOOK:

A History of Money and Banking in the United States: The Colonial Era to World War II. Auburn, Ala.: Ludwig von Mises Institute, 2005.

INDEX